Dream Mysteries

Secrets to Interpreting your Dreams to Know God's Purpose for Your Life

Lisa M. Kohut, Ed.S., M.Ed.

Table of Contents

Introduction

Dreaming, like the thought process itself, is something we're deeply intrigued by and something most of us can do, but rarely can we vividly remember dreams after we've had them, let alone make any sense of the scattered, often unconnected images we see while asleep. Everything is real in dreams, and nothing is sacred. In dreams we have harrowing experiences, from flight and graphic sex to death, even murder. And though we may want to, most of us can't predict what we'll be dreaming of from one night to the next. While some have learned how to control their dreams via the technique of Lucid Dreaming, even they don't have full control over their dreams, and when they do, they don't have it for very long. As with most subconscious acts, we've yielded all control. In the case of dreams, we're either watching or experiencing; we may enjoy the dream

3

or feel horror; it may feel like a lesson, or a warning, or even encouragement. We are free to focus on the pure emotion in dreams because from a control aspect, dreams often feel off-limits. We're the audience in our own private and mental short film, and there's nothing to do but sit back for the show.

In the Bible, Jesus teaches us how to pray and tells us that God knows what you will pray for before you ask for it. Even if you don't pray for it directly, you may still be asking God for help. Let's say that you hate your job, or let's go a step further and say that you hate your job so much a feeling of *dread* comes over you when you think about it after waking up in the morning. Six months ago, your kindly, sympathetic boss retired and a demanding, abrasive assistant manager took his place. Hypothetically, while your dreams have been different each night for the past six months, they all have a single recurring trait: at some point in these dreams, you fly. Flight is a common theme in dreams, with many more interpretations than most other elements of dreaming, but flying is most popularly considered to be an individual's subconscious perception of the amount of freedom he or she has in life. When you dream of flying, you are truly dreaming of freedom. In your dreams, if you fly low, or you never get off of the ground, it means something is holding you back. If there are obstructions in your path as you fly, these might represent the boss whom is standing in your way.

Let's continue with the new boss analogy. Seven months after the promotion of this new boss, you are promoted and transferred to another office where *you* are the boss; now free from the oppression of a bully-boss, you don't dream about flight quite so much anymore, or when you do, you're soaring; maybe even with wings. There's a deeper meaning to this interpretation besides a subconscious desire for freedom. God has worked through your own mind to tell you that on a conscious level, you weren't happy with things in your life. While you did not realize this and ask God to free you, God freed you himself in His usual mysterious and glorious way. Imagine all the things God could be telling us through our dreams but that we can't understand or interpret!

For Christians, dreams take on a special meaning they may not have for others. Our adherence to the words of the Old and New Testaments, and our exaltation of God and His Son, Jesus Christ, all leads us to the knowledge that God is always watching us, always communicating with us, and, if we allow it, always interacting with us. My hope is that this book will inspire you to look at your dreams as a more active part of your life instead of as a passive part of your life. My prayer is that you will begin to acknowledge God's Holy presence even as you sleep, and that you will be empowered enough to use the symbolic messages of your dreams to activate your hopes, goals, and purpose in life while you're awake. Most importantly, I hope that you enjoy the contents of this book and that you gain an understanding of the meaning of your dreams, because dreams can be a tool to help us guide our lives. Please note, although I mention Christians, this book is not intended for "Christians Only," but it is for all dreamers who have come to the understanding that dreams are another form of communication and who would like to explore this form of communication.

Chapter One

The Dream that Changed My Life

On June 10, 2000, I had a dream that changed my life. I had been praying and fasting in an attempt to experience God in a way that I hadn't experienced Him before, asking Him to manifest the gift of the Holy Spirit and any other Spiritual gifts that He wanted to bless me with.

I dreamed that I was pulling fish out of my throat. When I woke up, this bothered me because I didn't know what it meant, and I assumed that it was not good. You have to admit that it is a very unpleasant image! Immediately, I got on my knees and began to pray. I asked the Lord to reveal to me what this dream meant.

How did I know the dream was from Him? I knew because my Spirit was troubled, and the vision of the dream was so vivid that I couldn't shake it. Such a startlingly real dream could only have come from Him. After I prayed, I had faith that He would reveal the meaning to me.

That same evening, while I was talking to my friend Audra on the phone, something happened that changed my life and my walk with Christ forever. While Audra and I were talking, the Holy Spirit gave us revelation through Audra, who began speaking in tongues to interpret my dream. She began to pray for me to speak in tongues as well, but it wasn't happening.

Through Audra, the Holy Spirit told me to yield or surrender. I wasn't sure how I wasn't yielding, so the Holy Spirit told me to get in a humble position. I got on the floor on my stomach (the most humble position I could think of), and about two minutes later a flowing stream of unfamiliar words began to come out of my mouth. I was overwhelmed with joy, peace, love, revelation, and wisdom. I felt immediately cleansed of any baggage that had been in my soul. While I was in that position and speaking in the unfamiliar yet Holy language of tongues, I understood that I had received the gift of dream interpretation, and the Holy Spirit began its instruction with me by interpreting my own dream.

The Holy Spirit revealed that my dream had manifested in such a way so that I would understand how God was preparing me to use my vocal chords to save the souls of many men and women by giving them the Lord's wisdom. I knew that the ancient symbol of the Fish symbolized the renewal of the souls and spirits of men and women and the conversion of their souls to the Lord, but I didn't clearly understand (at least then) that a person's soul must be open and receptive for their Spirit to be fed. This is where dream interpretation comes in. I believe that many people who wouldn't otherwise be receptive to giving their life to the Lord become more receptive after having a dream that they can't shake and hearing the interpretation of that dream.

Immediately after having this dream and receiving this revelation, I began to be approached by people who were eager to share descriptions of their own dreams, and the Holy Spirit gave me revelation on those dreams without any effort whatsoever. The Holy Spirit also often gave me new information about the person that was related to the dream, information which I would have had no way of knowing without his divine influence. This surprised a great many, who were fascinated at the wisdom the Holy Spirit revealed to me. After speaking with me, they were often relieved and able to walk away in a calmer state of mind, knowing what their dreams meant.

Although dreams and visions are not new to mankind, dream interpretations are a bit more complex. God has been communicating with mankind through dreams and visions from the beginning of time, starting with the Old Testament, continuing through the New Testament, and even today. The words "dream" or "vision" appear in the Bible more than two hundred times, and the Bible recorded many encounters of men and women having dreams and visions. There are also many references to specific dreams in the Bible (we will touch upon those in later chapters).

Throughout this book, I will discuss the origin of dreams; some of the purposes of dreams; and why we should listen to our dreams even in the present day. I will also cover the true power behind dream interpretation and other spiritual gifts; some of the more common dream symbols with which everyone should be familiar; how to journal your dreams to capture the important components, thereby making it easier to interpret your own dreams; and the seven steps to interpreting your own dreams.

I will also explain three basic principles one should apply when interpreting dreams; step-by-step examples of previously interpreted dreams; and explanations of exactly how I interpret them myself, in that step-by-step manner. Finally, I will explain how to re-enter your dreams to further expand your revelation and interpretation of dreams.

WHAT IS THE DIFFERENCE BETWEEN DREAMS AND VISIONS, AND HOW CAN WE DETERMINE ONE FROM THE OTHER?

When God speaks to us through dreams, our dreams tend to be more personal and symbolic in nature. In other words, the messages that are conveyed to us in dreams are typically not what they *appear* to be. In Numbers 12:6-7, God speaks to Moses, Aaron, and Miriam: *"Listen to what I say: If there is a prophet among you from the Lord, I make Myself known to him in a vision; I speak with him in a dream."* This simply means that the message being communicated through *visions* tend to be much simpler and clearer, so that the individual receiving the vision knows the meaning directly upon receiving it.

Whereas God makes Himself or the message known in a *vision, dreams* tend to be much more symbolic. The scripture states that He speaks with the prophet in a dream. This means that God uses dreams to open our channels of communication; however, the message is not as clear as it will appear in a vision. It takes more soul-searching to be able to interpret dreams.

So, you may ask yourself, why would God use symbols when they are so complex and hard for people to understand? Why wouldn't He just give us all visions or speak to us clearly in a way that doesn't require solving any puzzles? God uses both forms of communication to talk to His children, and each is for a different reason. I believe that He speaks to us through dreams for the same reason that He spoke in parables in the Bible. In Mark 4:11, when his disciples asked Jesus why He speaks in parables, He replied, *"To you it has been given to know the mystery of the Kingdom of God, but to those who are outside all things come in parables, so that seeing they may see and not perceive, and hearing they may hear and not understand lest they should turn and their sins be forgiven them."*

In Biblical terms, the word "mystery" refers to something that has been previously hidden, but can be revealed through divine revelation. The Greek word for mystery comes from "mueo," meaning "to initiate into the mysteries," and "musterion," which refers to knowledge that is withheld, concealed, or silenced. Jesus conveyed the message that believers have the ability, through the Holy Spirit, to understand mysteries. However, it is expected that believers will initiate or seek an understanding of mysteries on their own. Individuals who have closed their eyes to the truth of the Spiritual realm will not understand the importance of this wisdom and will not seek or initiate the mysteries. Consequently, they will not be open to changing their thinking patterns and behavior from their old ways in order to live a blessed life.

Although not everyone will immediately be able to understand what God tries to convey to us when He speaks, He would like everyone to have the *desire* to understand what He is speaking of and thereby initiate the revelation of the mysteries.

Again, it may seem like a mystery at first, but as we search, seek, and ask, the mysteries will be revealed; we will find the truth, and our lives and our relationship with Jesus Christ and one another will be transformed. In Mark 4:22-23, Jesus says, *"There is nothing hidden which will not be revealed, nor has anything been kept secret, but that it should come to light. If anyone has ears to hear, let him hear."* God's intention is not to keep things away from us indefinitely or to hide them forever; His intention is to create a craving, a hunger in us that will lead us to seek His truth. His truth is for those with the heart to seek it out, not for those who despise the truth or aren't ready to receive it. For example, when I had my first life-changing dream about the fish, I was determined to find the meaning, which lead to the realization that I had the wonderful gift of dream interpretation.

If a dream provokes us to seek His truth, this will enhance our relationship with Him, which will then cause us to search for and seek Him. This is His ultimate desire. In Matthew 6:33, we are bidden not to worry ourselves with our clothes, or food, or our bodies: *"But seek first the kingdom of God and His righteousness and all of these things shall be added to you."* If our heart desires to only seek God's way of doing things, His purpose for our lives, His will for our lives, and His calling on our lives, He will bless us with all the things that our heart desires, including material goods, relationships, health, etc., without effort and without our need to search for them. The key to earthly blessings (material wealth, fulfilling relationships, peace of mind, good health, and so forth) is revealed as we seek out

His mysteries.

The key to living a fulfilling life is to seek out God's mysteries by being quiet and still so that we may hear His voice daily; being obedient to what He tells us to do; reading His word to establish the path we must follow; and relying on the Holy Spirit for guidance and teaching. God uses a plethora of tools with which to provoke us to search for His Kingdom, because it benefits us and pleases Him when we do so. He wants us to receive the benefits of seeking His Kingdom and to understand the language of heaven. In Matthew 6:9-10, when Jesus is speaking to the disciples and telling them how to pray, He says, *"In this manner, therefore pray: Our Father in heaven, Hallowed be Your name. Your kingdom come. Your will be done on earth as it is in heaven."* To truly apply the laws of heaven to our lives on earth, we must seek out the mysteries of heaven, because God's language is heavenly language. This heavenly or Spiritual language is not a language "of the world" or "of man." It is not a language that those who are accustomed to the world should understand or know, either. Heavenly language is only for those who are equipped to handle, deal with, and apply this level of wisdom. Those who are filled with the Holy Spirit typically have the desire to learn this language and are hungry and disciplined enough to search it out. They will also be equipped to handle it. God downloaded heavenly knowledge and wisdom onto our Spirits, but we have to go inward to access it. We have to take the time to be still, pray, and read the Bible to draw out the treasure that is already inside of us. The treasure inside of us is free, accessible, and valuable, but it takes faith, patience, and vision to access it. God wants everyone to have the desire to be one with Him;

for everyone to have the desire to understand and to seek out the symbols in their dreams. Once people act upon this desire and seek to understand his divine mysteries, only then will we be able to access such heavenly information.

In this book, my goal is to help and equip those of you who have the desire to search for and seek the meanings of your dreams and the everlasting mysteries of God.

Chapter 2

The Origin and Purpose of Dreams

Dreams have been a mystery to man since the beginning of time. Dreams have held many captive and awake at night, wondering if what they have just "seen" is reality or simply their imagination working overtime. We have all awoken from dreams disappointed that it wasn't reality, and conversely, we all know what it's like to wake up and thank God that a terrible nightmare wasn't a reality.

There are several different theories about the meaning, origin, and purpose of dreams. First, we will briefly discuss the origin of dreams. Although this book will address dreams that are Spiritual in origin, dreams come from three different sources. Dreams can be Spiritual in nature, or come from God; they can be of our soul's nature, or come from our own mind, will, and emotions; and they can be evil, coming from darkness. The false, or dark, dreams are typically in black and white, while the other dreams are in color.

I believe that dreams have several different purposes. One is to help us work out our subconscious issues while we sleep, and in this way, dreams serve as an extension of our subconscious. We may dream about things that we think about or activities that we are engaged in throughout the day, whether we are aware of it or not. This brings unresolved issues that we may need to work out to our attention. For example, one time when I was very overwhelmed with my responsibilities and everything that I had to get done, I wrote out a to do list before going to bed. After going to sleep, I dreamt that I was going on the Oprah Winfrey show and I didn't know what I was going to talk about. In the dream, I had a few hours before I was scheduled to appear on the show and I was asking people what I should talk about. This was an example of how my thoughts and unresolved issues of feeling overwhelmed during the day, was brought to my attention while I was asleep.

Another practical purpose of dreams is to restore our minds and bodies while we sleep. The stage of sleep during which this occurs is called REM sleep, or rapid-eye movement sleep, the deepest stage of sleep. Dreams also allow God to communicate with us and send us different types of messages while our minds are "turned off" and we are unconscious to the physical world. Although each purpose is important in its own way, for the purpose of this book, I will focus on the reasons that God uses our dreams as a form of Spirit communication. Because I don't believe that every dream that we have is from God or even God attempting to communicate with us, this poses the question: How do you know which dreams are from God and which ones aren't?

This is difficult to answer because there is *no* scientific answer to this question, and many people want a scientific, concrete answer regarding how to tell whether their dreams are from God. In the world of Spirituality and faith, sometimes the concept of "fact" or "reason" or "proof" is contradictory because knowing something by faith is different than knowing something due to facts. With faith, there are sometimes certain "unknowns," which is the very essence of faith. Faith is believing in something even though you haven't seen physical evidence or proof. Let's say you have a dream from God, and your inner voice may signal to you that this dream *meant* something.

Likewise, your Spirit may be unsettled or troubled when you wake up, like Nebuchadnezzar's Spirit after he had a dream from God. In Daniel 2:1 it states, *"Nebuchadnezzar had dreams, his mind was troubled and he could not sleep."* I believe this was his Spirit communicating to him that there was a message in his dreams for him, and maybe for others, as well.

In Daniel 7:15, Daniel states that after having a dream in which he was troubled in the Spirit, the visions that passed through his mind disturbed him.

I don't know about you, but when I've had dreams that I believe were from God, the same thing has happened to me. I recall the dream sometimes vividly and sometimes faintly, but regardless of how well I remember it I'll often feel unsettled afterwards, as if something needs to be resolved in my Spirit.

God spoke with many different individuals in their dreams. He spoke with Solomon, Abraham, Nebuchadnezzar, Joseph, and Daniel, to name just a few. However, even after establishing that God does, in fact, communicate with us through our dreams, you still may be wondering why.

WHY *DOES* GOD COMMUNICATE WITH US THROUGH OUR DREAMS?

I believe that God has six purposes for communicating to us through our dreams, and that it is up to us, along with direction from the Holy Spirit, to discern this purpose.

But before I talk about the purposes of dreams, I would like to say why I believe God uses our "dream time" to communicate with us. First, He attempts to communicate with all of us during our waking hours; however, because we are so busy, constantly moving and being affected by external stimuli, we very rarely take the time to be still and to listen to Him. So, often, God is there, speaking to us, but He just can't get our attention! Therefore, being the faithful God that He is, He takes the time at night. In Job 33:14 it states, *"For God may speak in one way, or in another, yet man does not perceive it."* This is God's natural, loving nature; God is faithful and willing to use whatever method it takes to get through to us. When we're sleeping, our minds are open and receptive to receive information; there are no distractions. This makes it a perfect opportunity for Him to download any type of symbol or vision onto our Spirits that He knows will get our attention, and often, that's exactly what happens.

Whether the dream is positive and for our

encouragement or perceived as a warning, dreams get our attention. The dream categories included in this book may help you identify the type of dream you have and let you know what type of action you may need to take.

Although I will be going over six purposes here, I certainly don't believe that these are the *only* purposes of our dreams; however, the ones listed here are some of the main purposes that I believe that God uses to communicate with us.

✝✝✝

THE PURPOSES

The first purpose of our dreams is **intercession**. I believe that God uses dreams to reveal things that are going on in our lives or in the lives of others to call us to intercede and pray for these people and about these particular situations. If we have a dream about someone or something that we know is not positive, and we don't know the interpretation of the dream or we don't know the person, we can still pray immediately and begin to intercede for that person or situation, because prayer changes things.

The second reason or purpose of our dreams may be to **warn us**. God may want to warn us about a direction we're headed in or about a decision we're about to make that may be outside of His will or purpose and that could lead to destruction. For example, one dreamer who was about to get married had a dream that when she was at the altar, there was a very bad storm. There were other components to this dream, but this dreamer took the storm in this dream as a warning and the wedding was canceled. Shortly after the wedding was canceled, specific things about this dreamer's ex-fiancé were revealed, which confirmed her decision. Another example is in the Bible. In Genesis 23, God came to Abimelech in a dream and warned him about Abraham's wife. Abraham had been dishonest about his wife Sara; he had said Sara was not his wife, but his sister. Therefore, Abimelech was going to take Sara for his wife before God revealed the truth to him through a dream and warned him not to touch her. Abimelech decided to heed God's warning and did not take Abraham's wife. However, if he *had* decided to disobey God, he would have had to face the natural consequences of his decision. God also demonstrates this kind of warning in Genesis 31:24, with Laban, Jacob's father-in-law. Laban had been dishonest with Jacob, and Jacob decided to flee after he was told to do so by God. When Jacob fled, Laban became upset and chased him. God then appeared to Laban in a dream and told him *"to be careful that you speak of*

Jacob neither good nor bad." Laban followed God's instructions; although he wanted to hurt Jacob, he did not.

God loves us and wants us to heed His warnings when we are headed in directions outside of His will. When we are headed in a direction leading to destruction, or when we're about to make a decision that will have negative consequences, God wants to intercede. In Daniel, Chapter 4, God gives Nebuchadnezzar a dream to warn him, as well. King Nebuchadnezzar is warned in his dream that if he does not acknowledge that God is more powerful than his own power and riches, his power will be taken away from him. Nebuchadnezzar's warning was to acknowledge and turn to God or lose his earthy privileges. Because Daniel, a godly man, interpreted this dream for him, Nebuchadnezzar had the opportunity to take action to avoid disaster and calamity in his life. God gives us the same opportunity if we heed His will and are obedient.

Job 33:14-18 states: *"For God may speak in one way, or in another, yet man does not perceive it. In a dream, in a vision of the night, when deep sleep falls upon men, while slumbering on their beds, then He opens the ears of men, and seals their instruction. In order to turn man from his deed, and conceal pride from man, He keeps back his soul from the pit, and his life from perishing by the sword."* While we sleep, God opens our ears and our hearts to hear His instructions regarding how to get out of a sad mess we may be in and to protect us from digging an even deeper hole. When we are unconscious, there is no pride to defend us from the truth, so it penetrates directly onto our hearts. This is why it's so important to search for the mysteries of your dreams.

The third purpose of dreams from God is to **give us**

hope and encouragement. In Proverbs 13:12, it is written: *"Hope deferred makes the heart sick, but a longing fulfilled is a tree of life."* You may be experiencing a dark time in your life and be tempted to throw in the towel and give up. But God may give you a dream to show you the light that lies ahead to give you a hope for your future. Having a visual image of a dream that He births in us gives us the opportunity to think about and hold on to that vision when things aren't going the way we planned. For example, during a time when one of my sisters was feeling discouraged about the course of her life and her purpose, she had a dream that she and her husband and her kids visited a beautiful home with many unexplored rooms. There was a lady there who had a lot of wisdom and many gifts that amazed them all. This dream was about my sister, and it was the Holy Spirit showing her all of the things that she already possesses that she hasn't tapped into because she wasn't acknowledging these gifts. Also, God gave Jacob a dream of encouragement when he was in a very distressing time in his life—running from the wrath of his brothers. Jacob lay down for the night in the wilderness and used a rock for a pillow. While he was sleeping, he dreamed of a ladder reaching from heaven to earth, with the angels ascending and descending at the top of the ladder. Jacob saw God in all His glory. This dream was an encouragement to Jacob during a very distressing and discouraging time in his life. God promised to be with Jacob on his journey and to prosper him and eventually get him back home safely. When Jacob woke up, he was utterly shocked that he had an encounter with God. Jacob then built an altar in remembrance of that day.

God then did the same thing for Gideon, when he

was going against the Midianites. God instructed Gideon first to diminish his army significantly so that when he won, God would get the glory. In a dream, he was instructed to go down to the enemy's camp. While Gideon was there, he overheard someone describing a dream and discerning its interpretation, which was that God was going to deliver the Midianites into Gideon's hands. This encouraged Gideon and gave him confidence and faith that he was ready for battle.

The fourth purpose of dreams is to **give us confirmation** about something that He either has already tried to communicate to us through our Spirit or through someone else or something that we've asked for confirmation about. Again, this is a very acceptable and easy mode of communication that we get when we sleep, and it doesn't leave us until it's served its purpose.

36

Another, fifth, purpose of our dreams is for **prophecy**—to tell us of things that will come to pass. This kind of dream can come to us on a broader level and is not confined to our own lives or our families' and friends' lives, but may involve information regarding the nations, cities, and states in our world. In the prophetic books in the Bible, such as Amos and Daniel, prophecy is discussed rather thoroughly. In the book of Daniel, for example, God speaks about four beasts that are symbolic of four future powerful kingdoms. God used these prophets to record these prophecies so that we could also experience and know what is to come if we are able to comprehend what we read.

Also, in Genesis 37:11, God gave Joseph dreams about what was to happen in the future regarding his father and his brothers, and how they would end up bowing down to him several years to decades later. This dream did come to pass in Joseph's life.

God also gave a dream of prophecy to Joseph, Mary's husband. When Mary was impregnated by the Holy Spirit, God gave Joseph a dream to prepare him for the role that he would play in Mary's life and in the life of Jesus to prepare him and so that he would know that Mary was truly pregnant with God's Son.

I also believe that God communicates with us in dreams simply to let us know that He is God. It's hard not to believe in His power when He uses dreams to communicate with ordinary people like Daniel and even me. But when God gives us dreams, it is our responsibility to search out their meanings and to understand their purposes, and then put them to action in whatever manner that we believe God wishes. If God calls us to pray, it is our responsibility to pray, and if He is calling us to use the dream prophetically and share it with someone, it is our responsibility to listen intently to the Holy Spirit and to carry out that purpose. Sometimes God even asks us to keep the dream to ourselves. We must search out the meaning of the dream and understand it, even if we need to rely on someone else until we become more confident in interpreting our own dreams. Visual images are powerful and often not forgotten, so when God gives us these visual images, it's His way of ushering in the positive Spirit to replace the negative, worldly images in our subconscious. If we are thinking about negative things, sometimes He will give us these images to show us that these hindrances are blocking us from getting our heart's desires. He wants us to have our heart's desires, and He's willing to communicate with us in any way that he can in order to fulfill this for us and help us to get closer and closer to Him.

Chapter 3

Love: The True Power Behind Dreams

Using the Eyes of Our Heart to Maximize the Gifts of the Spirit

1 Corinthians 13:1-3 *"If I speak the languages of men and of angels, but do not have love, I am a sounding gong or a clanging cymbal. If I have the gift of prophecy, and understand all mysteries and all knowledge, and If I have all faith, so that I can move mountains, but do not have love, I am nothing. And if I donate all my goods to feed the poor, and if I give my body to be burned, but do not have love, I gain nothing."*

Sometimes we are so intrigued and mesmerized by

41

the development of our spiritual gifts as we watch them grow that we forget about one of the most basic yet most critical parts of those gifts, which is love. Sometimes we get so caught up seeking and expressing gifts that we forget about the impact that our words and actions have on our loved ones.

Love, expressed in our relationships with others, is the foundation of every gift that we could ever hope to manifest. Our relationship with others is a reflection of the depth of our love for God and ourselves. If we don't love God and we don't love ourselves, it is less likely that we will treat others with love. After all, the Bible says, *"Love your neighbor as yourself."*

Unfortunately, as powerful as it is, the love component of our Spiritual gifts is often excluded when we are being taught about how to use our gifts. I want to take some time to discuss the importance of love before, during, and after the use of our gifts. As stated in 1 Corinthians 13: 1-3, we can have the most powerful manifestations of the gifts of the Spirit, but the power will fade and eventually be meaningless if we don't operate from a place of love. Our gifts will be much more powerful and will have more impact on those to whom we minister when we live a life with a testimony of love. We will also have many more opportunities to utilize our gifts, because people want to receive insight, wisdom, and direction from people who they sense love them and are non-judgmental toward them.

HOW CAN WE ACTIVATE THE POWER OF LOVE?

Perhaps you've been asking yourself, "Why aren't my gifts growing?" Or, "How can I continue to develop the gifts that God gave me?" Or even, "What am I doing wrong?" The answer could be simply that your "love walk" needs to be developed more thoroughly. If your family, friends, or co-workers see you as judgmental and unapproachable, you may be walking down the wrong road to demonstrate and activate your love walk. Do people see you as a comforter, or an accuser? As someone who is more likely to condemn and blame, or to forgive? Are you merciful, or adversarial and argumentative? Would they describe you as a gossip who talks negatively about people, or an encourager who builds people up and edifies them?

We aren't expected to be perfect, but we ought to have the desire to be like Jesus, who was and is Love. Our first ministry is to our family and loved ones, and when we pass this test, He will entrust us with more. The Holy Spirit made it very clear to me that in order to use my Spiritual gifts, I had to use and exercise the "eyes of my heart." The eyes of my heart are my Spiritual eyes—the eyes that see beyond the physical and allow me to see others in the same light in which God sees them—flawless. God doesn't view us as physical beings, but as Spiritual beings. In the Spirit, we are perfect in His sight. If we penetrate people's shells and get to know them beyond the surface, or ask God to help us use the "eyes of our hearts" to see people instead of the eyes of our flesh, we will begin to experience growth in the Spirit and in our Spiritual gifts.

The "eyes of our hearts" are tender and have sensors of compassion, love, truth, and light. This is where God stores wisdom and mysteries, so that when we are exercising His true power and seeing others with love and compassion, He reveals mysteries and revelation to us. For example, when I'm allowing the Holy Spirit to use me to interpret dreams, I am not using my physical eyes to discern what the dream means; instead, I am using the eyes of my heart, which reveals mysteries and secrets that my physical eyes can't see.

Paul prays in the book of Ephesians 1:18, *"The eyes of your understanding being enlightened: that ye may know what is the hope of his calling, and what the riches of the glory of His inheritance in the saints."* Paul is calling on us as believers to use the eyes of our Spirit, the eyes that we perceive with and imagine with, to cause something to exist and come to light that may not already exist! When we use the eyes of our mind to create or illumine the existence around us, we will begin to see what we desire to see with our *physical eyes*, and we will fulfill the excellent expectations to which God has invited us. He is calling us to have bright hopes and to begin to understand what He has invested in us.

This concept is simpler than it sounds. It entails

seeing others and their futures with our imagination, which includes a shining hope, and when we speak of this into the lives of others, they will begin to allow their imaginations to be directed to this light of hope as well. For example, one day when my sister and my two nephews were riding in the car, one of my nephews (William) said, "Aunt Lisa, you know what I want to be when I grow up? I want to be a scientist." I looked at William's eyes and said, "William, I can totally see you being a scientist, but you know what else I see? I see you being an inventor. You will invent something that will help millions of people one day." William gazed at me as my words registered in the fibers of his belief system, and he said, "Yeah." I knew from the look on his face that he received the words that I spoke in his heart, and he was allowing them to direct his imagination.

The very next day, he began to name and identify invention ideas, and up to this day, at eleven years old, he "invents" (writes and creates) comics. This is a perfect example of how the power of using the "eyes of our understanding" can enlighten others to walk into the hope of their calling. When we are enlightened, we enlighten others, and the more of us that are enlightened, the better this world will be.

HOW DO I KNOW WHEN I'M USING THE EYES OF MY HEART?

I believe that it is critical for us to know the truth in every situation in our lives, so that we can expose the lies that create darkness and keep us from living up to our full potential. In John 8:32, the Bible says, *"You shall know the truth and the truth shall set you free."* When Jesus was asked, *"Which is the greatest commandment in the law?"*

48

he summed it up with two words—love and relationships. Jesus said, *"You shall love the Lord your God with all your heart, with all your soul, and with all your mind."* And *"You shall love your neighbor as yourself."* Everything else in our lives, including our gifts, should build on these two basic principles. We need to love God, ourselves, and our neighbors. We need to show love in every relationship that we have, starting with God. It is not possible for us to prosper in every area of our lives, including Spiritually, emotionally, physically, mentally, and financially, without prioritizing these principles. However, the power and importance of love is often underestimated in the lives of believers. That is why I have included the above explanation, supported with scripture, regarding how to use the eyes of our hearts: so that the Holy Spirit can help us use the eyes of our hearts in our relationships and convict us when we aren't. The point is not to condemn anyone or cause feelings of guilt, but to propel us to higher levels and to encourage us to seek the best in our relationships and, ultimately, in our gifts.

When I'm using the eyes of my heart, this means I have confidence in God's character, which is Pure and Holy. He doesn't have the same limited perspective that we have. Rather, He has a comprehensive perspective of our character, because He can see our hearts and the hearts of others and therefore does not overemphasize our behaviors or actions. In I Samuel 16:7, when God instructs Samuel to replace Saul with another King due to Saul's disobedience, God's character and view become transparent. When Samuel uses the eyes of his flesh and is tempted to select Eliab based on his external appearance (tall and handsome), the Lord said, *"Do not look at his appearance or at his physical stature, because I have refused him. For the Lord does not see as man sees, for man looks at the outward appearance, but the Lord looks at the heart.*" To truly exercise the use of the eyes of our hearts, we must detach ourselves from the addiction of evaluating others and ourselves based on external appearances.

As humans, we see others and assign our own value to them based on our previous experiences, messages, or beliefs and exclude the truth, which is that we were all created in God's image. He called us all "good," and everything that He created is considered "good." So when we accept Jesus, we become One with the Most High and One with each other.

What separates us from God and from others is the deceptive thinking that we are superior or inferior to anyone else God created. Our values—the highest and the lowest, and the best and worst, are all judgmental in nature and based in egotistical pride. When we feel detached, separated, disjointed, or inferior to others, we have the temptation to act out of fear, hatred, judgment, anger, and competitiveness. When we view ourselves as inferior to someone else, we try to find someone to whom we feel superior, because that is the way the ego works. As long as someone is inferior, that means someone else is superior; and as long as you feel inferior, it's difficult to build others up and genuinely use the eyes of our hearts.

We were not created to operate as islands. If we were, there would only be one person on the planet! When we feel alone, the dreadful, fearful ego takes control and begins to chastise, judge, hate, and compete. How do we know that we are supposed to be operating as One? Jesus, the great Master, said, *"I and the Father are One."* and

Jesus said, *"Whatever you did to the least of these you did to me."* This applies to us as well—whatever we do or say about others, we are also doing and saying about ourselves. This is the law of "sowing and reaping." We can't think a negative thought about someone, treat someone badly, or feel a negative emotion toward someone else without it adversely affecting us. Science is proving with quantum particles that even though they appear to be disconnected, they act as if they *are* connected. We are the same—all connected, all as one. This may be a difficult reality to face, but the more our minds (and physical bodies) are blocked with hatred, fear, guilt, judgment, anger, etc., the more difficult this will be to digest. Since we are all connected, then no one is truly inferior or superior, and realizing that God sees us all the same, as His perfect creations, will help banish the hatred and fear that sometimes can cloud the eyes of our hearts. Using the eyes of our hearts the way we were created requires making a conscious decision and being disciplined. It requires using self control to consciously look inward when we're most tempted to look and evaluate outward.

WHAT IF WE HAVE DARKNESS IN OUR BELIEF SYSTEMS AND THOUGHTS, AND WE DENY IT OR DON'T KNOW IT?

Eventually, this sense of darkness will manifest itself in the body and Spirit in some way, through ill health, unhealthy and toxic relationships, our finances, and so on. We can't escape the messages we send out. As 1 John 5 says, our body, relationships, emotions, and finances can only be in good health if our soul is prospering, and our soul can only prosper if we are filling it with things that are true, noble, just, pure, lovely, and of good report (Philippians 4:8). This includes a diet of edifying or building others up in our thoughts, words, and actions.

When I am using the eyes of my heart, I am looking at imperfect and broken people (including myself) with compassion and love and seeing them the way God sees them—perfect, whole, and in the presence of His light. I work in a therapeutic day school with children who have been identified and labeled as "emotionally or behaviorally disturbed." By the time these children get to me, many of them have adopted and internalized the lie that they are useless, unworthy, hopeless, and failures. In many cases, they have been told these lies verbally and nonverbally by trusted adults like their parents, other family members, or even school personnel, and they have begun to act out these lies.

The wrong image affects every decision. When the children come to me, I know that in order for me to see any progress in their academic or behavioral, emotional, and

Spiritual functioning, I must find a way to change and

correct the internal distorted image that they have of

themselves. In order for me to change their image of them,

I must make sure that my image of them is not what I may

have seen in their files, in their behaviors, or in what I may

have heard from their previous schools or even their

parents. Instead, I must look at their hearts and see them the

way their precious Father sees them. I must look beyond

the physical into the Spirit and see that this child was

created in the Image of Christ, this child is mighty and

powerful, but he/she doesn't know it yet, so he/she is acting

out of fear. I do what it says in John 7:24: *"Do not judge*

according to appearance, but judge with righteous

judgment."

From that vantage point, I begin to see the students

from a different perspective, and then I begin to interact with them differently. When I interact with them differently, I speak to them differently, and before you know it, I begin to see them behave differently academically, emotionally, and behaviorally! It begins with the decision to use the eyes of our hearts—by looking beyond what we see on the outside, even when it looks ugly—and choosing to see the beauty, speak the beauty, and interact with the beauty until it manifests.

When I am using the eyes of my heart, I am relying on supernatural wisdom to create an image in my heart that I can't see in the flesh. This requires faith and love. Hebrews 11:1 says, *"Faith is the substance of things hoped for, the evidence of things not seen."* In other words, faith creates substance and provides evidence for things that we have prayed for even before they physically manifest. The only way that we can create substance before it manifests is with the eyes of our hearts, which is to use our imagination in love.

Certainly we have all used our imagination in a self-serving way (such as seeing ourselves in the home or car or relationship of our dreams), but have we exercised these same muscles enough to see others the way God wants us to see them? Seeing someone in a different way than they are acting requires a lot of faith, and it is an action of love. However, it is one of the most powerful things that we can do in our relationships, and it truly changes people.

We must begin to consider ourselves developers of potential. Potential simply means hidden abilities. Our abilities are hidden behind fears and lies that we have believed, and our job is to go into the world and use our imagination and our tongues to change people's potential from impotent to potent. Potential comes from the word "potent," but so many of us aren't potent because we have allowed such negative beliefs in our lives. We must place a demand on others' potential so that they become what they are capable of becoming as their potential is challenged—and God gets the Glory.

When I am using the eyes of my heart, I am using my tongue and my imagination to create hope, life, and purpose in the lives of others. This principle reinforces what I spoke about previously in terms of seeing others differently than they may be behaving and, consequently, interacting with them differently and using the powerful force of our tongue to speak hope and purpose into the life of others. This is the foundation of the gift of prophecy. The gift of prophecy is so powerful because it edifies people and gives them a visual image to hope for in their future. When people don't feel like they have a purpose or an image, they give up and lose hope and begin to behave negatively. Proverbs 18:21 says, *"Death and life are in the power of the tongue and those who love it will eat its fruit."* Simply by speaking words of encouragement, hope, and life, we have the power to be the life support for those who are hanging onto life by threads.

Words are Spirit, and they don't die—they just get replaced. We can choose to plant words of truth and hope in the minds of those with whom we interact so that when they are in a critical or compromising situation, they can rest on the words of Spirit and make a fruitful decision.

In my life, my mother has spoken with more words of hope and encouragement than any other person I know. While I was growing up and facing stressful situations or decisions, I would often hear my mother's words: "I know you can do it; you can do anything," or "You're so intelligent." These words would echo in my mind when I was making decisions from peer pressure to being disciplined. I believe that aside from God's hand being on my life, it was my mother's confidence in me and her loving yet confident way of expressing it that saved me from the temptation of drugs, alcohol and other snares of the enemy.

Again, when I am using the eyes of my heart, I realize that there is no such thing as inferiority or superiority—God created us all equal because we are one in Christ. 2 Corinthians 10:12 says, *"For we dare not class ourselves or compare ourselves with those who commend themselves. But they, measuring themselves by themselves, and comparing themselves among themselves, are not wise."* We can't use our own standards to compare ourselves to others or classify ourselves because in doing so, we would be commending someone falsely. Jesus spoke in John 17: 21 *"that they all may be one, as You, Father, are in Me, and I in You; that they also may be one in Us, that the world may believe that You sent Me."* This is a prayer for unity. The only way that we can have unity on this earth is to believe that we are all created equally and that our differences complement one another, not separate us from one another.

Jesus called for us to be one with one another as He is with His Father, so that we could also be one with Him. Jesus did not act without first getting permission from His Father, and He did nothing against His Father's will, even if it was difficult or painful. If we behave in this same manner toward one another, where we seek God's face to guide our thoughts and actions about one another, we will

62

truly be acting out Jesus' commands of loving God and loving one another as we love ourselves.

When I am using the eyes of my heart, I am facilitating unity, life, and an atmosphere in which it is safe and free for others to grow. When we eliminate our attitudes of inferiority and superiority, we eliminate attitudes of judgment. This is a very good thing, because judgment creates an atmosphere of fear. In Luke 6:36-37, it says, *"Therefore be merciful, just as your Father also is merciful. Judge not, and you shall not be judged. Condemn not, and you shall not be condemned. Forgive, and you shall be forgiven."* We have all needed mercy before and will continue to need mercy; therefore, we must be merciful in our relationships, thoughts, and attitudes with ourselves and others. Our attitude of mercy, love, fairness, and unity will create an inviting atmosphere where people will feel free and safe to share their mistakes and confess their sins, which brings healing and forgiveness.

Also, this attitude extends that same grace to us when we make mistakes. Galatians 6:1 instructs us on how to intercede when we see a brother or sister falling into sin: *"Brethren, if a man is overtaken in any trespass, you who are spiritual restore such a one in a spirit of gentleness, considering yourself lest you also be tempted."* We must approach one another in the same spirit of gentleness that Jesus approached the woman at the well who had committed adultery. He did not approach her with condemnation or judgment; instead, He approached her with love, which gave her the power to walk away from sin. This is the same manner in which we must interact with one another. We must eliminate our attempts to expect those around us to live up to standards that we know we haven't lived up to ourselves. Who do we think we are, anyway? We must remove the fairy tale that when we are judging or comparing our mistakes to the mistakes of others that we are righteous and good or better than them because we haven't done anything as "bad" as they have. This attitude is rule- and law-based and separates us from love. Galatians 5:4 speaks to this by saying, *"You have become estranged from Christ, you who attempt to be justified by law; you have fallen from grace."* When we fool ourselves into believing that anything that we do "good" is apart from God and that we are capable of being good without God, we separate ourselves from God and His grace. Furthermore, we must be careful about what we judge, because we attract what we judge, which is what Luke 6:36-37 states. Often, when we judge or look down at someone due to their sins or negative behavior, we end up seeing the same sin in our own lives— either directly or indirectly. 1 Peter 4:8 states that *"Love covers a multitude of sins."* If we really want to see change in our lives and the lives of those around us, the force that will most likely bring about this change is love. Love covers sin—not judgment, condemnation, berating, or gossip.

When I am using the eyes of my heart, I am under God's grace and operating in faith through love, which replaces the law. Romans 8:1-2 states: *"There is therefore now no condemnation to those who are in Christ Jesus, who do not walk according to the flesh, but according to the Spirit. For the law of the Spirit of life in Christ Jesus has made me free from the law of sin and death."* This means that the law of love replaces the law of perfection. We accept Jesus Christ in our hearts because we realize that we have no chance at being perfect without Him. We realize that by lying, cheating, stealing, gossiping, and any other sins, we are unable to be perfect on our own. Therefore, by accepting Him, we are no longer held to the human standard of perfection, but we *are* held to God's standard of grace. We realize that once we truly understand His love, it increases our faith and replaces our unrealistic expectation of perfection. We replace it with the power of the Holy Spirit, which guides and instructs us on what to do every minute and every day of our lives if we listen. It gives us the strength to be excellent and live according to God's standards and grace. This is walking according to the Spirit, not according to the flesh.

When we walk according to the Spirit, we don't condemn ourselves or others, which weakens the flesh. When we live according to love, we fulfill the law of love and do right by God and others. This is confirmed in

Galatians 5:1314: *"For you, brethren, have been called to liberty; only do not use liberty as an opportunity for the flesh, but through love serve one another. For all the law is fulfilled in one word even in this: You shall love your neighbor as yourself."* We create liberty when we love one another, and we create bondage when we judge.

I am valuing love and revelation over knowledge and information when I am using the eyes of my heart. I Corinthians 13: 1-3 says: *"If I speak the languages of men and of angels, but do not have love, I am a sounding gong or a clanging cymbal. If I have the gift of prophecy, and understand all mysteries and all knowledge, and If I have all faith, so that I can move mountains, but do not have love, I am nothing. And if I donate all my goods to feed the poor, and if I give my body to be burned, but do not have love, I gain nothing."* This scripture speaks to the fact that it doesn't matter how impressive our gifts are; if we are not operating in love, they will not reap rewards for us or others. In many cases, if we are not walking in love, people will have a difficult time receiving Spiritual gifts from us or believing that they are truly from God. If you think a certain person doesn't like you and he gives you a material gift, it is much more difficult to receive it from him, because you wonder about his motives or if he is truly sincere. I think it's the same way with Spiritual gifts. It is always much easier to receive anything from someone whom we like and believe likes us and walks in love than it is to receive from someone who is suspect.

If your relationships are broken, first seek to repair them before seeking to increase in your gifts. It is difficult to be in communion with God when our relationships with His children are in disarray and we are not attempting to repair them in love. The best way for our gifts to be magnified, utilized, and increased is for us to be in communion with the Holy Spirit and hearing God's voice in our everyday affairs and relationships, and then in our call to ministry in blessing others.

Chapter 4

Common Dream Symbols

Obviously there are thousands, probably even millions, of dream symbols, and there's really no way to memorize all of them. My goal in this chapter is not so much to exhaust all the symbols, but to really review them in a way that will help you familiarize yourself with some of the most common ones. These are mainly symbols from dreams that I've interpreted and noticed as being common, so again, this is not to be an exhaustive list, but just a start.

Hopefully, this will help whet your appetite and allow you to become more familiar with some of the most common symbols. I recommend getting a Christian dream dictionary if you do want a more extensive list. Again, it is important to keep in mind that every individual has his own dream "language," so although there are some common, universal dream symbols, there is no such thing as a one-size-fits-all dream symbol. God communicates with all of us differently.

Also, it's important to note that some of the symbols have more than one meaning, depending on the context of the dream. For example, **animals** in general typically represent your emotions, so if you dream about an animal that you feel uncertain of, you may ask yourself what emotion the animal may represent to you, depending on the type of animal and the expression of the animal in your dream.

Before we start, I have one more very important instruction. While interpreting dreams, it's always good to begin with the understanding of the *origination* of the dream. In other words, was the dream soulish (related to your soul)? Were you thinking about or meditating on something throughout the day that was related to your dream? Was it a nightmare or in black and white, indicating that it came from the dark realm? Or was it a dream in which the Holy Spirit was trying to communicate a message to you? Determining its origination is vital to determining its meaning. Now, let's jump in with a few select categories!

ANIMALS

Birds often represent the Holy Spirit, evil spirits, or wicked rulers, depending on the type of bird. The **Dove** is often symbolic of the Holy Spirit, peace, and a new beginning, while **Black Crows** may be symbolic of harassers or mockers.

Cats could be symbolic of curiosity or deception, while **Cats and Dogs** can symbolize the individual's relationship with people. In other words, if you dream about cats and dogs fighting, this could by symbolic of discord in your personal relationships with others. In a dream about a cat or dog, it's important to note the *type* of cat or dog and how you relate to it within the context of the dream. For example, a friend of mine had a dream about two black cats with blood shot eyes fighting in front of her window, a few weeks prior to being betrayed by her friend and boyfriend. This particular friend has a black cat of her own that she adores, which is probably why black cats were used as a symbol for two people that she really cared about. Another example may include dreaming of fancy show dogs, which may mean that you put too much stock in appearance and false finery. For **Dogs**, it's also important to know whether the dog is a biting dog or not.

Additionally, dreaming of a bloodhound tracking you may be a warning about the danger of falling into temptation. For **Dogs**, it's also important to know whether the dog is a biting dog or not. For example, several years ago, when I was going through an IRS audit for real estate, I had a dream of an animal that looked like a cross between a dog and a wolf. The animal had sharp teeth, and I was initially afraid of the animal. During the dream, I realized that although it had sharp teeth and it could hurt me if it decided to bite me, it was a friendly animal, and I befriended it. When I woke up, I realized that this dream was symbolic of my relationship with the auditor who had been assigned to my case for the audit. Initially, I was feeling like she was my enemy, but the Holy Spirit was showing me that she was not my enemy and that I would gain favor with her if I let my guard down. I obeyed and began to look at her differently after this dream. After I changed my response to her, I noticed that she became more friendly and helpful and the rest of my audit went very smoothly. Thank God for dreams!

Fish are symbolic of people's souls, newly saved souls, and clean and unclean spirits. Fish are also symbolic of mass provisions of food or provisions in any form.

The **Lion** is symbolic of the enemy (Satan) and persecution. **Snakes** are often symbolic of Satan, deception, criticism, and gossip. **Spiders** often symbolize enemies, whereas **Eagles** could symbolize freedom. **Ants** are symbolic of unwanted guests, or hard work; **Bees** are symbolic of gossip or attacks; **Elephants** are symbolic of strength and wisdom; and **Pigs** can be symbolic of something unclean that could lead to destruction.

NUMBERS

The number **One** represents unity and new beginnings; **Two** is symbolic of witnesses or testimony; **Three** is often perfection or witness; **Four** often represents the four corners of the world or the globe; **Five** is responsibility or grace; **Six** is often symbolic of man and the beast; **Seven** is completion, **Eight** is new beginnings; **Nine** is judgment or finality, and **Ten** is order.

DIRECTIONS

East is often symbolic of beginning, a first experience, or birth; **West** is last, the end or death; **North** is often symbolic of something Spiritual, Heaven, or Spiritual warfare; and **South** is symbolic of the world, temptation, trials, and the flesh.

Pregnancy is often symbolic of a new beginning or new ideas, and it may mean literal pregnancy or growth. **Police or Security guards**; are often symbolic of angels, demons or a Spiritual authority, including pastors or elders and protection. **Buildings** are often representative or symbolic of the individual dreamer, the church, classrooms, or other places of teaching or learning; and to dream of a **Garden** is often symbolic of a harvest of reaping and sowing, the dreamer's life situation or heart. A **Hospital** is symbolic of a place of spiritual healing; a **House** is symbolic of the soul, or the individual who is dreaming. (It is usually important to pay attention to whose house one dreams about; though your house represents you, often if you dream about someone else's house, it could be reflective of your relationship with that person. It is also important to pay attention to the time period of the house that you dream about. If you dream about a house from the past or from your childhood, your dream may be telling you about something that may be still affecting you, but that occurred when you were younger.) A **Basement** is usually about things hidden, things that are stored underneath the subconscious; an **Attic** is usually the mind, thought, or attitude; and a **Bathroom**, including the **Shower**, **Toilets**, and **Bathtubs**, is a place of repentance and usually indicates cleansing. A **Kitchen** is a place of preparation, usually for teaching or for Ministry. The **Bedroom** is a place of rest or ease in personal life, and intimacy; the **Backyard** represents the past and things behind the person; the **Front Yard** is often symbolic of the future and things ahead; and **Vehicles** are usually symbolic of a Ministry or a person's life. (It is important to pay attention to the type of vehicle, the size of the vehicle, who is driving, whether you're in the front seat or the back seat, and all of those details.) A **Bicycle** would be a ministry or life that might be struggling or is causing a lot of toil, energy, or effort; **Dancing** is worshiping; **Eating** usually symbolizes agreements or covenants, and **Falling** is usually fear. (This could be a falling into sin or old bad habits, depending on the type of falling and where and what you are falling into.) **Flying** typically symbolizes the ability to overcome certain circumstances or obstacles; **Rain, Water,** and **Swimming Pools** are usually symbolic of the Holy Spirit, Spiritual activities, or gifts of the Spirit being used. **Hair** is covering or tradition; **Teeth** is wisdom, information, or experience; a **Clock** or **Watch** indicates making changes, particularly where time may be an obstacle; **Stairs** depend on whether they or you, in the dream, are going up or down. (Going up could indicate that you're increasing in abundance or literally "moving up," and going down could signify depression or regressing Spiritually or physically, depending on the context of the dream.) **Clouds** are storms; **Eyes** are the window to the heart; or the desire or ability to see in the Spirit; **Feet** are shoes or a person's walk with God; **Fire** is trials and burden, persecution; and **Flowers** indicate the flesh and the desire for things of the world. **Money** is about natural talent to be converted into wealth; **Tornado** or **Storms** are great trouble or the sudden disturbance or Spiritual warfare.

Being **Naked** or **Exposed** is often symbolic of becoming transparent, vulnerable, or humbled; **Sudden Death** could be symbolic of a sudden life change; dreams of **Being Chased** or **Chasing** are symbolic of enemies that are at work, coming against your life and purpose, or something that frightens you. **Clothing** typically represents covering, mantle, or calling; a **Coat** is symbolic of protection or insulation; and **Ribbons** may be symbolic of reminders.

Roller Coasters may be symbolic of instability; **Different Rooms** may be symbolic of different issues that you may be experiencing in various areas of your life (again, consider the room, and what it represents to you); **Crops** may be symbolic of seed or season; dreams of **Doors** or going through doors is often symbolic of change that is coming or options and opportunities that may be on their way; Dreams of **Relatives** who are deceased could indicate generational issues (curses or blessings) that have been passed down; dreams of **Past Relationships** are often symbolic of the temptation to fall back into old thinking patterns or habits, and dreaming of a past relationship that you have fond memories of could indicate God's desire to restore good things, feelings, or times in your life.

Again, these symbolic meanings are only suggestions and may vary widely, depending on the context of the dream. Each symbol potentially has several possible meanings. Also, whenever dreaming of people, in addition to looking at the context, it's important to identify what the individual represents to you.

Chapter 5

Dreams about Colors

Common Dream Colors and Their Meanings

Have you ever wondered why some of your dreams

are in color and some are in black and white, or why you

remember the colors of some of the symbols in your

dreams while you forget others? The colors in your dreams

are significant, and this chapter will explain their various

symbolic meanings. Although the same color can have

different meanings in different dreams, colors usually tend

to have general themes and specific meanings. Throughout

this chapter, I will explain the positive and negative

meanings of some of the most common colors we dream

about.

WHITE

The color white appears often in many dreams. When you have a dream that has a symbol with the color white, it typically symbolizes the Spirit of the Lord, purity, and righteousness. White is also often associated with light in scriptures.

Although the color white is generally associated with good, this is not the case when the dream is about people. When dreaming about people, it's always important to discern the context.

RED

Red is another common dream color. Although red has many meanings depending on the context of the dream and the symbol that it is attached to, it can mean wisdom, anointing, power, passion, the Blood of Jesus, and sacrifice if it appears in a positive context, and anger, war, and deep sins if it appears in a negative context.

BLUE

Blue is another common dream color that has positive and negative meanings. When blue is dreamt about in a positive sense, it symbolizes the Holy Spirit, heaven, communion, or revelation; when dreamt about in a negative context, it could symbolize depression and anxiety.

YELLOW

Yellow frequently appears in dreams, as well. Yellow is often symbolic of the mind, hope, or honor in a positive sense, and fear, infirmity, and sin in a negative sense.

BLACK

Black is the last frequently dreamed about color. Black typically symbolizes darkness, sin, ignorance, and the judgment of God. Dreaming about people who are black or white does not typically symbolize the people being positive or negative, unless the dreamer has positive or negative beliefs about a particular race, then the dream could symbolize the dreamer's thoughts or beliefs about that race or individual. it's important to pay close attention to the context of the dream. For example, one dreamer, who happened to be white, had a dream about going into an all black church to speak. Before speaking, the church showed a video of him on the screen and he perceived himself to look like a "hillbilly" and got embarrassed and left the church before speaking. This dream revealed the dreamer's sensitivity to cultural and external differences and fear of being judged based on these differences. This was a dream to encourage the dreamer to focus on the "unseen," not what he could see, or he may potentially miss out on God's calling for his life.

OTHER COLORS

You may also dream about **Brown** or **Tan** symbols (symbolic of being without spirit or repentance); **Orange** symbols (danger, warning, or caution); or **Purple** symbols (wealth).

†††

Although this list doesn't exhaust the colors that may appear in your dreams, it does share with you the colors you will most likely see after you drift off to sleep. It is very important to rely on the Holy Spirit to discern the meaning of the color and to consider the context of the dream. When doing this, it is important to consider the personal life situation of the individual having the dream before applying any of the meanings of the dreams. If the person is experiencing a struggle in his or her life, then the colors may have a more negative connotation. If the person is in a very happy place, then it is more likely that the colors have a positive meaning. Remember, please use the above descriptions as a guide and not as a one-color-fits-all formula when interpreting dreams for yourself and others.

Chapter 6

Dreams about Parts of the Body

Many people have dreams about different parts of the body. Typically, these dreams indicate that the body part is important by exaggerating the size, color, shape, etc. of the body part or by simply making the body part memorable in some way. Again, it's important to remember that the context of the dream and symbol is always important when interpreting dreams; however, for the purpose of this book, I will focus on the general symbolic meaning of some body parts that have come up in dreams.

Eyes symbolize the means of seeing or the window to the heart and soul. If you dream about yours or someone else's eyes being closed, it may indicate slumbering, being unaware of what's going on, a state of ignorance, or purposefully refusing to see something. Ask the Holy Spirit to open your eyes or the eyes of anyone that are closed if you have this dream.

The Face often symbolizes the nature or identity of someone. If you dream about a face or even another person, it's important to pay attention to the expression and mood or to ask what that particular person represents to you. In other words, what is the first thing that comes to mind when you think of that person?

The Belly symbolizes a person's spirit, feelings, or desires. In dreams about the belly, you want to pay attention to what is inside of the belly, or what came out of the belly. If it's water or something that indicates life, that is a good dream, but if it's something that indicates evil, ask the Holy Spirit to change the desires of your heart. John 7:38 is an example of the belly being used to describe the spirit.

91

Dreaming about a baby inside of the belly could symbolize a new idea that is in the development stages or a new season of your life. On the other hand, dreaming about something like wood being in your belly could symbolize being full of flesh or worldly desires (lust, etc.).

The Hand symbolizes a person's spiritual strength or power. In dreams about hands, you want to pay attention to what the hand was doing or whether the hand appeared to be strong or weak, as well as whether it was the right or left hand. For example, one dreamer had a dream about her daughter's left hand being in a very pretty cast. This dream indicated that her daughter was using something that appeared attractive to cover up her spiritual strength. In other words, there was something compromising or handicapping her true strength. The right hand symbolizes natural strength and the left hand symbolizes spiritual strength.

Feet symbolize a person's walk with God, as well as their ways, heart, or thoughts. Dreams about feet can be complex, and the dreamer should pay attention to things like whether the feet were bare or not, whether they were strong, and even where they were headed.

Bowels symbolize the seat of our emotions. When we dream about our bowels or feces or urinating, we need to pay attention to the context, where are we, who else is around, and the feeling we have at that time. Again, particularly with these types of dreams, feelings are very important, because dreaming about the bowels is often communicating something about our emotions. For example, one dreamer had a dream that he was at a public location and lost control of his bowels before he made it to the bathroom, and he was embarrassed. This dream indicated that the dreamer lost control of his emotions in a way that was unpleasant to him and those around him, before he could repent (reach the bathroom) or regain control.

Chapter 7

Dreams about Falling or Being Chased

Dreaming about falling or being chased can be very revealing but very traumatic. Many people have recurring dreams of falling or being chased; they wake up relieved to find that it was a dream, but frightened because they don't know what it means. The good news is that dreams about falling or being chased are actually a chance for enlightenment. They may be revealing some of our anxieties and insecurities that we are experiencing while we're awake, but that we're avoiding or refusing to confront. Either type of dream indicates that there is something in life you need to attend to before your Spirit can feel peaceful once again.

Dreams of falling often reveal a fear of being out of control or overwhelmed in some area of our lives, areas we're not aware of or that we're not addressing. The feeling of not being in control or feeling overwhelmed could be the result of losing some type of support, including emotional or financial, or you could simply be enduring a time of great trial. Again, it's always important to pay attention to the context of the dream. In other words, from where are you falling? What are you falling into? Who's around or not around? For example, falling from a mountain could symbolize a dreamer's fear of losing power and control in a particular area of his life. It's very common for children to have falling dreams. One child was having reoccurring dreams of falling off a cliff, which indicated that there was some area(s) of uncertainty or instability in this child's life that was causing her fear and anxiety. Stability and certainty are very important to children, so even the slightest bit of uncertainty can throw them off. This dream could also indicate that there has been some type of emotional trauma that she has not recovered from. Again, context is very important.

A dream in which you are being chased can be equally unsettling. Being chased often reveals feelings of anxiety that the dreamer may be experiencing while being awake. The chaser or pursuer is often another aspect of the dreamer. It could be an uncomfortable emotion like anger or fear that hasn't been dealt with, or even negative thoughts that are tormenting an individual. If you have a recurring chasing dream where you're being chased, do the following:

1. Pray before going to bed and ask the Holy Spirit to reveal who or what is chasing you.

2. Decide before going to sleep that you're going to confront the chaser in your dream, so that you will confront the chaser in your life.

3. Decide before going to bed that there is nothing to fear.

4. Read Psalm 91 each night before going to bed. This is a powerful and comforting scripture that has helped many people overcome fear.

Chapter 8

Dreams about Marriage

Many people have dreams about marriage, including getting married, being a bride or a groom, or even about their current spouse. The Bible states in Ephesians 5:31-32: *"For this reason a man shall leave his father and mother and be joined to his wife, and the two shall become one flesh. This is a great mystery, but I speak concerning Christ and the church."* This scripture compares the marital relationship to Christ's relationship with the church, which is typically what dreams about marriage symbolize; in our dream, we are the church (individually and corporately) and the marriage indicates that we are entering into a union with Christ. In other words, dreaming that you are a bride often means that you are the bride of Christ. One person recently had a dream where many different people were entering his bedroom, and it was interfering with his sleep and intimacy with his wife. In this dream, his wife symbolized Christ, and the different people were symbolic of the different distractions that were coming against his attempts to have an intimate relationship with God. Often, a person's current spouse or past spouse is used in dreams to symbolize Christ. Marriage can also symbolize entering a covenant of some type. The covenant could be a literal marriage, a church, or even an agreement or business relationship with someone. Overall, it's important to remember that dreaming about your spouse doesn't necessarily mean that your spouse literally represents the person that you're married to, and dreaming that you're getting married doesn't necessarily mean that you are getting married in your waking life. Remember to rely on the Holy Spirit and the context of the dream for the

interpretation.

Chapter 9

Dreams with Sexual Content: R-Rated Dreams

Dreams about sex can take on many different meanings and interpretations, depending on the context and the original source of the dream. Since dreams can originate from your soul, spirit, or the dark or demonic realm, it is definitely important to discern which of these sources the dream comes from before attempting to interpret the dream. We discussed earlier how to discern the origin of dreams, so in this chapter, I will primarily discuss the dreams of sexual nature that originate from the spirit realm.

It is very common for people to assume that a dream with sexual content automatically indicates perversion or something negative. Although this can be true sometimes, it is definitely not always the case. Obviously, because dreams can often be an extension of the dreamer's subconscious, dreams with sexual content can simply reveal certain physical desires or temptations from the dreamer's soul. However, spiritually there are many more possible interpretations. Dr. Joe Ibojie mentions in his book *Dreams and Visions* that sex in a dream may indicate that a person is making or about to make a decision based on the flesh. He also mentions that in the Bible, sexual immorality symbolizes unfaithfulness or deviation from spiritual truth, or even a stronghold of lust that may be hidden. For example, dreaming about being raped could indicate that the dreamer or the rape victim's person or integrity is being violated. A dream with sexual content including the dreamer could also be a warning that the dreamer needs a cleansing of attitudes of the mind, motives of the heart, or acts of immorality.

In a more positive light, dreams with sexual content could also be symbolic of a spiritual call to greater intimacy with God, your calling, or your purpose. An example of this would be dreaming about having sex with your spouse or a spiritual leader. Another possible meaning of sex in a dream could be a joining or union with a specific person or group. Although this union would not be sexual, God could be telling you that you will be developing a higher level of intimacy with this group or person. Another explanation for having sex in a dream could be to show the dreamer possible areas of vulnerability in her life as a result of strong fixations or preoccupations, either conscious or unconscious, that he or she may have with attitudes or people from the past. For example, a friend of mine had repeated sexual dreams of her ex-husband. She was concerned because she didn't feel like she had any desire to be with him when, as a matter of fact, she was struggling with unforgiveness toward him. Her dream was revealing negative thoughts and memories of her ex-husband and her past that she was allowing to inhabit her mind. This preoccupation with the past and the feelings of unforgiveness were obviously contaminating her thought life and needed to be cleansed. The unforgiveness was keeping her connected to her ex-husband in a way that she no longer wanted to be connected to him,, which was affecting many other areas of her life as well.

Although dreams with sexual content are by no means limited to these explanations, this chapter is a good foundation to use when interpreting dreams with sexual content.

Questions to Consider when Interpreting Dreams with Sexual Content:

1. Is the person having sex with the same sex or the opposite sex? This could indicate whether you're sowing into the lives of those like you or into the lives of those that are different than you.

2. Are you and others naked in the dream? Being naked is symbolic of transparency, which God views as a good thing.

3. If it's an individual, is it an old or a new love? Sometimes this indicates whether you're passionate about things from the past or present.

4. Does this person or group replace the Lord or add to your relationship with Him?

5. Finally, how do you feel upon waking up?

Chapter 10

Dreams about Death

Dreaming about death or dying can be a traumatic experience, whether the dream is about you or someone else who you know and love. We often wake up relieved that it was a dream, but still shaken up and frightened that it may come true. We are left wondering what the dream may really mean; since to many of us death is a scary subject, we assume that it could not possibly be good to dream about it. How can a dream that leaves us upset herald something positive?

The good news is that dreams about death are not typically negative. Usually, when people in the Bible talked about death, it was symbolic for the flesh. When Jesus was crucified, he died in the flesh and was resurrected. This very action symbolized our victory over sin and death, once our corporal body dies (the flesh, ego). The flesh is our selfish and fearful belief systems and thoughts that lead to ungodly desires, temptations, and actions that separate us from God and His Will for us. In I Corinthians 15:31, Paul mentions that he dies daily. Obviously, he didn't die literally, but he had to put his flesh to rest, which means that he puts all his sins and temptations behind him. Our flesh may also be put to rest through persecution, attacks, criticism, or humiliation by others. The very things that we hate the most and that feel the worst are the very things that help us to be closer to God. Putting your flesh to rest means laying down your worldly self and focusing on the Spirit.

In Hebrews 2:14, the scripture refers to Jesus Christ destroying death and the power of the devil with the crucifixion and the resurrection. Thus, death in a dream symbolizes the end of something, or something without

life. It could mean that someone has died to a particular

type of sin, which would indicate that the person has

freedom from the power of sin or the works of the flesh. A

dream of death may also symbolize the end of a difficult

season of someone's life or the end of a church without life.

However, an ending doesn't have to be negative, as we

have discussed; symbolic death is just a chance for a new,

more Spiritual beginning. There are some occasions when

death does indicate literal death; however, this would be

considered a prophetic dream or vision and this is rare. The

most important thing to remember is that the context of the

dream and the Holy Spirit must be used to help you to

interpret the dream.

Chapter 11

Dreams from the Dark or Demonic Realms

Remember that when attempting to interpret your dreams, it is important to understand the origin of the dream. Dreams can originate from the dreamer's soul, which just means that the dream is reflecting the individual's thoughts, feelings, or experiences. These dreams may also reveal areas of our soul that need to be healed or things that are going on in the subconscious that we may not be aware of consciously. Dreams may also originate from the Holy Spirit or God, and those dreams typically give us some type of direction, warning, or edification; and some dreams may originate from the dark realm or demonic forces. I will briefly discuss how to know when dreams originate from the dark or demonic realms and what to do with them once you have them.

First, it is important to acknowledge that the dark realm counterfeits anything from the light realm and attempts to use it to cause fear, confusion, and separation from God. Since the images in dreams are extremely powerful, it is critical that we are able to discern when this is happening. Due to the power of the visual images in dreams, including dreams from the dark realm, it's easy to mistake these dreams as messages from the Lord and allow them to influence us to take negative actions in our lives that can be destructive to our lives and the lives of our loved ones.

CHARACTERISTICS OF DARK OR DEMONIC DREAMS

The first and most obvious type of dream that comes from the dark realm is what one would consider a nightmare. Some nightmares can also be considered "soulish," that is, relating to the soul; however, most nightmares are likely from the demonic realm. Dreams that are demonic are often in black and white or have very little color. The colors that are present are usually dark or subdued, as opposed to the bright and vivid colors that are in dreams from the Holy Spirit or from the dreamer's soul. These dreams also typically consist of ominous and unfamiliar symbols that make the dreamer feel uncomfortable. These symbols and colors often trigger negative emotions in the dreamer.

The emotions that the dreamer feels immediately upon waking up are another indicator of the origin of the dream. This doesn't mean that every time you wake up alarmed the dream is dark, but if the colors are blunted or dark and you wake up filled with anxiety, fear, or other negative emotions, it could be a demonic dream. The Bible says in I Timothy 4:1: *"Now the Spirit expressly says that in latter times some will depart from the faith, giving heed to deceiving spirits and doctrines of demons."* This verse indicates that deceptive spirits will be active in the last days and will cause some people to walk away from their faith. I believe that one way these deceptive spirits will attempt to deceive us will be through our dreams, attempting to enter our minds to cause confusion and burden us with fear and anxiety, which causes many to turn away from God's plan for their lives. The goal of deceptive dreams is to influence us to make poor decisions related to finances, sexuality, relationships, career, parenting, and the church.

You may want to ask yourself the following questions when determining if the dream you've experienced has a dark origin.

1. Was the dream in black and white or color?

2. Were my emotions positive or negative when I woke up from the dream?

3. And finally, does the dream tempt me to do something that may not be good for me or that goes against the Word of God?

HOW TO RESPOND TO DARK DREAMS

First, recognize that the dream is from the dark realm. Next, ask the Holy Spirit to reveal the root or origin of the dream. Finally, pray the Blood of Jesus over your dreams, bind any tormenting spirits, and ask the Holy Spirit to heal your soul.

Chapter 12

Journaling your Dreams

Recording your dreams in a dream journal is a very critical and important step, because if you don't remember your dream, you have nothing to interpret! You could also be missing some very important information that God wants you to have. So by all means, write down or type or even voice-record your dreams the instant you wake up. Don't let too much time pass, but don't try too hard to remember, either; just make sure you have something close at hand to turn to when you awaken. In Daniel 7:1, Daniel wrote down his dreams by just describing the main facts.

Select and identify a journal that only *you* will use to record the main facts of your dreams. Put your dream journal and a pen (if you're going to write your dreams down) next to your bed and keep them there.

Also, before going to sleep each night, ask the Lord to speak to you in your dreams and ask the Holy Spirit to help you to remember the dreams when you wake up. Taking these steps will prompt the Holy Spirit to recognize that your Spirit is ready to engage in dialogue with God through your dreams and that you will take them seriously. I keep a dream journal and a pen on my dresser next to my bed to be prepared to write down the main facts of my dreams as soon as I wake up. This puts you in the mindset of expectation. When I have this journal and pen next to my bed, before I go to bed at night I'm basically saying that I'm expecting to have a dream that I will wake up and remember to write down. Also, by writing the dream down as soon as I awake, I am increasing the likelihood of remembering the main facts or important components of my dreams. Although it is not always important to record all of the details, it is important to record the significant information while it's fresh. Typically, the significant information is more vivid than the other information anyway. If you take these faith actions coupled with your prayer, asking for more dreams, this will activate your Spiritual dream life.

Another key to journaling your dreams involves how to record your dreams to make it easier for you or the interpreter to explain the meaning and examine the significance of your dreams. After writing down the main facts of your dream, it is important to **note your feelings** during the dream and upon waking up. There is no doubt that feelings are an important component in dream interpretation, and the feelings connected to the dream are easier to capture immediately following the dream.

You also want to break the dream into symbolic "parts," such as identifying the **setting of the dream** or the location; for example, where did the dream take place? Who were **the people** in the dream, and what is their relationship to you? What do they represent to you? Next, take special note of **the activities** in the dream—what activities were you engaged in, and what do these activities represent to you? Finally, make sure to record any other **symbols**, including objects, colors, numbers, animals, letters, names, and so on.

As you wrap it up, consider the overall theme of the dream—in other words, if you had to name it using one to three words, what would you name your dream, and why? This will help you get a "big picture" of the dream by summarizing it, and when you go through your journal later, it will be easier for you to make a connection between the dream and what was going on at that point in your life, or what God was communicating to you at that particular time.

Your last task should be to categorize the dream. Identify the purpose that you believe is being communicated through this dream, such as whether you believe the dream is from God or sent as a warning, encouragement, etc. Even if you aren't sure about the interpretation, often you can discern the intended purpose of the communication. If not, ask the Holy Spirit.

Finally, make sure to date each dream. This will be beneficial as time passes and you decide to look back to remember specific dreams or periods in your life. Certain dates are significant because they represent different seasons in our lives.

Chapter 13

Interpreting Your Dreams

In this chapter, we will attempt to break down the complexities of dream interpretation and simplify the process of dream interpretation as much as possible. As I mentioned before, dream interpretation is a somewhat complex and complicated process for those who are not necessarily familiar with the symbolic or Spiritual realm, and near-impossible for those who are not filled with the Holy Spirit. However, once one becomes familiar with the Spiritual realm, it is not very complex at all. In fact, it is very simple once you're able to understand that the Holy Spirit is doing all the work! However, you must still take some basic steps and employ the principles of dream interpretation if you want to get the most out of your dream-time experiences.

1)   Record your dreams. How to record your dream is up to you, as we discussed in the previous chapter, so I won't go into further detail except to reiterate that this is the first integral step in interpreting your dreams

2)   Familiarize yourself with the common dream symbols. Remember, the language of dreams is symbolic. When you're beginning to interpret your dreams, the dream language may at first seem foreign to you, and it might take time for your Spirit to get used to this different "language." The temptation will be to interpret the dream as face value or as it seems, but things being what they seem on the surface is very rarely the case in dreams. There are literally *thousands* of Biblical dream symbols, so I'm certainly not

suggesting that you memorize all of them, but I do hope that you'll become familiar with some of the more common symbols that come up in dreams. Soon, this will be a natural process. As you continue to look up the symbols in your dreams, you will become more and more familiar with the process. You may not even have to refer to this book!

Another way to familiarize yourself with dream symbols is to look at five to ten dream symbols a day, even if you have dreams that you don't remember. You can look up these symbols on a Christian online dictionary or in a bound book about Biblical symbols. It is very important to make sure you choose a Christian or Biblical dictionary, however, because many dream dictionaries do not use the Bible as the reference for the symbols, and your dream interpretation will not be accurate in most cases.

3)   Familiarize yourself with your personal dream
language. Certain, specific symbols will mean something
different to you than they will mean for another person,
because most symbols come from the dreamer's life and
are specific to his or her culture. There are also archetypal,
or universal, symbols, which have been found to have the
same meaning, regardless of the dreamer. However, each
dreamer has his or her own language. Therefore, it is
important to remember that when you interpret your dreams
by looking at the symbols there's no such thing as "one-
dream-symbol-fits-all." Of course, as I've discussed before,
the symbols' meanings will not be easily apparent at first;
while you will recognize their meaning in time, and then
understand them going into the future, you must still put
forth the initial effort in deciphering them.

Remember that the symbol can mean different

126

things to different people. For example, to one person the Holy Spirit may be symbolized by a dove, which is of course a common symbol for the Holy Spirit. Yet to another person, the Holy Spirit may be symbolized in their dreams as an invisible face. You'll begin to notice and interpret patterns when the same objects, places, people, etc., keep showing up in your dreams.

It's a little ironic that a "one-size-fits-all" dream does not exist, because its absence tends to make it more complex to interpret certain symbols and a particular dream language. But just remember: God loves us so much that He personalizes his communication with us! So by all means, be ready!

4)   Develop and nurture an intimate relationship with the Holy Spirit. According to the Bible, the Holy Spirit is our Counselor and our Guide, our teacher and our

comforter. I rely heavily upon the wisdom of the Holy Spirit when I'm interpreting dreams, and I honestly couldn't imagine doing it without the Holy Spirit.

However, before I began relying on the Holy Spirit to help me interpret dreams, I had developed a *personal relationship* with the Holy Spirit: I communicated with the Holy Spirit regarding everyday issues and concerns in my life, and I encourage you to pray for the gift of the Holy Spirit, as well.

In I Corinthians 14, the Bible talks about the gifts of the Spirit. We all receive the Holy Spirit when we accept Jesus Christ into our hearts. However, the power of the Holy Spirit didn't manifest in my life until I asked for and received the gift of the Holy Spirit, which manifested itself in me by speaking in tongues. (You can also read about this phenomenon in I Corinthians 14.)

So, in my case, I did not begin interpreting dreams until I began speaking in tongues, and the same night that I manifested the gift of the Holy Spirit by speaking in tongues, the Holy Spirit revealed to me that I have the gift of interpreting dreams. For me, speaking in tongues stores wisdom; once I got to know and become familiar with the voice and wisdom of the Holy Spirit, I felt comfortable with listening and knowing. James 1:5 says, *"Now if any of you lacks wisdom, he should ask God, who gives generously and without criticizing, and it will be given to him."* Apply this scripture to request wisdom when you begin to interpret your dreams. Before interpreting any dream, ask the Holy Spirit for wisdom by saying something like, "Thank you, Heavenly Father, for your Word in James 1:5, which says that I can ask for wisdom and you will give it to me generously. I ask you and thank you for wisdom for the interpretation of this dream, in the Name of Jesus."

Once you have spoken this prayer, have Faith and believe that you will have the ability to understand your dreams, as James 1:6 states: *"But let him ask in Faith without doubting. For the doubter is like the surging sea, driven and tossed by the wind."* Even if you don't feel like you have the right interpretation, believe that the Holy Spirit has revealed the mystery to you and that in time you will discern the correct meaning.

And though I've talked about how "we" interpret "our" dreams throughout this book, I have to laugh a little, because God is really the one running the show, so to speak; God Himself is really the one interpreting our dreams! However, it's important that we nurture an intimate relationship with the Holy Spirit; we have to get to know the voice and the wisdom of the Holy Spirit so that we will feel comfortable listening to it. Until we develop and establish this reliance on the Holy Spirit, it will be difficult for us to rely upon the Holy Spirit to interpret our dreams and others' dreams with confidence.

In my experience, for example, I first developed and nurtured a personal relationship with the Holy Spirit just like I would develop a friendship. I spent time with the Holy Spirit, asked the Holy Spirit for wisdom, asked questions, and just generally treated the Holy Spirit as my friend and confidante—after all, the Holy Spirit is *supposed* to be our best friend!

So, when you sincerely ask the Holy Spirit for advice and wisdom, you will begin to trust the wisdom and guidance of the Holy Spirit to a point where you will have internal peace, no matter what you're experiencing. The Holy Spirit will guide you to the truth. As the Bible says, the Holy Spirit guides us to all truth, as in I Corinthians 2:9: *"Eye has not seen nor ear heard nor entered into the heart of man things which God has prepared for those who love him"* The book goes on to say that God has revealed these things to us through His Spirit. No one knows the things of God except the Spirit of God.

✝✝✝

Now, we want to receive not the Spirit of the *world*, but the Spirit of *God*, so that we might know the things that have been freely given to us by God. These things we also speak not in words, but what the Holy Spirit teaches.

The worldly man is not receiving the things of the Spirit of God, for they are foolishness to him; he cannot know them because they are Spiritually discerned. This

132

reiterates how dreams are symbolic and how we cannot know their mysteries with our natural eye.

Remember, when God gives us dreams, often He is revealing mysteries—he is whetting our Spiritual appetites so we will seek these mysteries and the things of the Spirit that will bless us. He wants us to be closer to Him because it will bless us. And as we search out His mysteries, they will reveal things to us about the world that we live in and about how to endure it; how to get through certain things that worldly wisdom cannot reveal to us.

God searches the things of God through the Spirit. In other words, you cannot question psychics regarding a dream from God, and you cannot type your dream into a secular website forum to determine what God meant for you because, again, your dreams are distinctly personal. Sure, you might be able to get the interpretation through secular means, but that is taking a chance with your soul. Although there are times when secular advice may lead you in the right direction, for the most part, if you want an accurate understanding and comprehension of your dream, you need to seek the Holy Spirit.

I Corinthians 13 discusses how we speak not in words that man's wisdom teaches, but that which the Holy Spirit teaches. For example, when we say, "Natural man cannot receive the things of the Spirit of God," it means that we cannot understand our dreams just by thinking about them. We must not interpret dreams for ourselves and for others by using worldly knowledge, because such knowledge is foolishness. A person who doesn't understand the Spiritual realm cannot interpret dreams. Consider I Corinthians 2 -15, which reads: *"The person with the Spirit makes judgments about all things, but such a person is not subject to merely human judgments, for 'Who has known*

the mind of the Lord so as to instruct him?' But we have the

mind of Christ."

When we seek out Spiritual wisdom, we are
entering into the mind of Christ, because Christ interprets
these dreams; we are only the "messengers," so to speak.

HOW DO I GO ABOUT DEVELOPING A RELATIONSHIP WITH THE HOLY SPIRIT?

This is an important question, because many people
either feel they are in tune with the Holy Spirit but are not,
and others *know* they are not but truly yearn to be, and they
want to know how to develop a personal relationship with
the Holy Spirit.

Here is a very specific example from James 1:5:
"Now if any of you lacks wisdom let him ask of God who

gives to all liberally and without reproach and it will be given to him. " You can use this scripture to request wisdom when beginning to interpret dreams or when you're looking for the answer to any problem and, like I said, I would start applying this in all areas of your life. Why not? The Holy Spirit *wants* to help you!

Likewise, when I speak to God, I say something like, "I thank you for wisdom in this situation. I thank you for giving me insight on where to go for a job. I thank you for wisdom in how to handle this situation. Thank you for putting the right words on my tongue to help this person understand his or her situation." These are just a few examples of how you begin to rely on and ask the Holy Spirit to guide you.

I also ask the Holy Spirit questions before I go to sleep, and I use this prayer from James 1:5: "Thank you,

Heavenly Father, for your Word in James 1:5. When I ask for wisdom, I ask that you give it to me generously. I ask you and thank you for wisdom for the interpretation of this dream, in the name of Jesus." Once you have spoken this prayer, have faith and believe that you have an understanding of the dream, as it says in James 1:6: *"But let them ask in faith with no doubting for he who doubts is like a wave of the sea driven and tossed by the wind."* In other words, even if you don't feel like you have the interpretation, believe that the Holy Spirit has revealed mysteries to you and just begin speaking or start typing.

I interpret many dreams via my dream website for people whom I have never met; I pray and believe that the Holy Spirit is giving me wisdom about these people. Again, I can't see with my natural eyes; I can't hear with my natural ears; and I can't understand it or conceive it with my heart but through love and with the Holy Spirit as my guide. The Holy Spirit gives me information about people through the Spirit that is stirred up in my heart. Develop a relationship with the Holy Spirit—it is so important! It will just bless every area of your life when you really adopt the Holy Spirit as your best friend. The Holy Spirit is within you and has all of the wisdom that you could ever need for any and every situation.

How Do I Seek Wisdom about My Purpose from the Holy Spirit?

There are several questions that you may ask the Holy Spirit while praying, journaling or before going to bed at night. When I ask the Holy Spirit a question before going to bed at night, I write down the question in my dream journal, ask it out loud before going to bed and I think about it or repeat it before going to sleep. The following are some questions that you can ask the Holy Spirit to obtain answers about your purpose.

- **What direction should I take in my life?**
- **What should I do about my current problem or situation?**
- **What is my purpose?**
- **Show me what I need to know now**
- **Reveal to me what I need to know to fulfill my purpose.**

These are just a few of the questions that you can ask the Holy Spirit about your purpose to send your Spirit searching for the answer to these questions either in your dreams or while you're awake.

5)   Break the dream down into parts.

Because dreams are often filled with symbols and

are very complex, it is important to break them down before attempting to interpret them, just as we discussed in Chapter Four.

6)   Look at the big picture and possible themes.

After breaking the dream down, look at the dream and themes it bears as a whole. Your dream journaling will help you with this step. Now it's time to put it all together, pray for guidance, and have faith as you interpret the dream.

Finally, make sure that any interpretation that you receive from yourself or others aligns with God's Word and agrees with your Spirit. The dreamer is the best person to interpret his or her own dream because he or she knows the intimate details of his or her life better than anyone else. Therefore, there will be less room for error if you're interpreting your own dreams with the guidance of the Holy Spirit. And it's very important to ask for confirmation before acting on your dream if you are uncertain. There is a great potential human error that can be involved in interpreting the dreams of others or prophesying over people. For example, let's say you received an interpretation that advised you to quit your job, and you quit your job without getting confirmation. Obviously, if the advice wasn't from God, or if the interpreter spoke in error, you could experience unnecessary consequences from making such a decision. Simply asking for confirmation can save many of us from a lot of heartache.

Chapter 14

Three Principles of Dream Interpretation

The first principle of dream interpretation is that your dreams generally reveal concerns of your heart or issues that have been present in the past two to three days. Ecclesiastes 5:3 states: *"For a dream comes through much activity."* In other words, it is not uncommon to dream about the activities of the day or previous days. You may want to ask yourself the question, What does this symbol mean to me? What significant issues have I been dealing with two or three days before I had this dream? Although dreams reveal issues of the heart, some of the issues may be from the past, so don't exclude the possibility of your dream revealing unresolved issues from even the far past. Before going to bed, you may want to begin taking note of

142

the things that you are thinking about, concerned about, praying about, etc., because it is very likely that your spirit will work some of these things out in your dreams. For example, I often ask the Holy Spirit for wisdom about specific areas of my life before going to sleep. I will write down a question on my dream journal and expect the Holy Spirit to guide me toward the answer. Without fail, the Holy Spirit always gives me wisdom, within time.

The second principle of dream interpretation is to remember that typically, any images, people, animals, objects, or symbols in our dreams are often facets of the dreamer's character, physical being, personality, or lifestyle. In other words, these symbols are often God's creative way of showing us things about ourselves, and they often don't represent what they appear to represent. God may use these creative images to reveal some of the intimate details of the dreamer's life. In other words, just because you dream about another person who you know, doesn't mean that the dream is about that person; instead it often indicates that He is using a facet of that person to communicate something to you. The fact is that most of the dreams that any dreamer has will apply specifically to the person having the dream, because the dreamer needs to have the position and authority to act on whatever instruction that is being given in the dream.

The third principle is that dreams are sealed instructions for the dreamer. We must understand the language of the Holy Spirit in order to successfully interpret the dream and apply the instructions of the dream. Job 33: 14-16 states: *"For God may speak in one way, or in another, yet man does not perceive it. In a dream, in a vision of the night, When deep sleep falls upon men, While slumbering on their beds, Then He opens the ears of men, and seals their instruction in order to turn man from his deed, and conceal pride from man, He keeps back his soul from the Pit, and his life from perishing by the sword."* If we are unable to receive instruction from God during waking hours due to our pride or inability to hear Him, He will subdue our flesh and open our spiritual ears to save our souls. God will attempt everything to help us to avoid the Pit.

Chapter 15

Interpreting Your Dreams Part II: Seven Steps

In this chapter, I will show you how to break down the interpretation process by re-examining dreams that I have interpreted. Because I can't break down the process the Holy Spirit reveals, that part is just implied. Inviting the Holy Spirit involves *thanking* the Holy Spirit for giving us wisdom, but we will break down the other parts before going into the final interpretation. So, I will share the dream that was given to me and break it down into parts, and then I will give the full interpretation of the dream.

Dream: This individual dreamt of a brick house with a brick wall and a little hole in the wall that they could see through. There was also a large back yard. The context of this dream was that the individual had been looking at houses.

Setting: A brick house and a back yard.

Symbols: After looking at the setting and the symbols, define the important symbols. A brick house is usually man-made, and the backyard usually symbolizes memories of the past.

Interpretation: The Holy Spirit revealed that this person was basically making the man-made decisions about his life by following his own will, and one of the things influencing him was that a part of the past continued to influence his current decisions. The hole in the brick wall indicated that this individual had some revelation about what he was doing; however, he continued to look into the past.

SEVEN QUESTIONS TO ASK

Symbols: What symbols were present in the dream, and

what do they mean in the context of the dream?

Emotions: Were there any emotions during the dream or upon waking up?

Actions: Were there any significant actions in the dream? How does this dream relate to what has been going on in the dreamer's life in the past two to three days?

People: Were there any significant people in the dream, and if so, what do they represent?

Setting: What was the location of the dream; where did it take place, and how is that significant to the dreamer?

Category: What category would this dream fit into?

Action taken: Does this dream suggest that the dreamer needs to take

any kind of action?

†††

Dream: This person dreamt that she was driving a car up a steep hill and while she was driving the car, she noticed flowers growing alongside the road in different places. She wanted to stop to dig up the flowers and plant them in the garden, but she didn't have the time.

Setting: Outside, driving in a car, observing flowers.

Symbols: Cars are often symbolic of ministry or a person's life. Flowers are often the flesh or worldly desires. The hill could be symbolic of difficult times or experiencing something that requires effort.

Interpretation: God was showing this individual that she is on a journey and would soon be in a Ministry, which was represented by driving the car. The flowers that this person wanted to stop and dig up represented the way that she was tempted with worldly distractions that she had been facing. The fact that this person did not stop indicates that she has overcome a lot of those desires and has been able to focus on her mission. The purpose of this dream was to give her encouragement that she does have the strength to focus on her goals and can accomplish them.

✝✝✝

Dream: This individual had a dream that they were in the back yard of their childhood home and heard a crying or wailing sound. He noticed that the sound was coming from a turtle that was giving birth to several baby turtles. The turtle was crying because the turtle had given birth many times before, and the babies would always die.

Setting: The back yard of a childhood home.

Symbols: Turtles crying and wailing, birth, and babies dying.

Interpretation: The childhood home is symbolic of a

period during this person's childhood or the past. Crying indicates grieving and feelings of distress, and turtles represent a slow process, or caution and prudence. Birth represents new ideas being born. Dying off is symbolic of new ideas dying off. The interpretation of this dream indicates that when this person was a child, he had a cautious spirit that caused him to approach things very slowly, which then delayed many things. That Spirit of fear or caution entered and began to influence this person as a child. The turtles represented the dreams of this person, and how they were going through a slow process. This person likely felt like his dreams, hopes, and God's promises had been very "delayed" in nature and, in many cases, had even been unfruitful. The turtles dying off were symbolic of the feeling that this person's dreams had been aborted or have not come to pass. The turtles' crying and wailing represents how this person feels about dreams that seemed to keep dying. The fact that there were still a few alive indicated that this person still had some dreams that were alive during the time and was hoping they would come true.

✝✝✝

Dream: This individual dreamt of her brother chasing her with a kitchen utensil.

Symbols: Chasing, kitchen utensil, and brother.

Interpretation: Dreams with the symbol of chasing often represent fear of enemies. The kitchen utensil would be symbolic of preparation, as in preparing food. The brother in this dream likely represents this person's brother, or, in other dreams, it could be a *characteristic* of someone's brother. This dream communicated this person's subconscious or conscious fear of her brother interfering with or destroying the preparation of her life.

†††

Dream: This individual had a dream that her teeth were crumbling and only remembered that when her teeth were crumbling she felt very upset. She remembered waking up feeling afraid and fearful.

Symbols: Teeth crumbling.

Emotions: Afraid and upset.

Interpretation: Teeth are symbolic of wisdom, experience, or knowledge. The fact that this person's teeth were crumbling in her dream indicates that she felt like she was losing something or at a loss in some way, or didn't have a certain type of wisdom or knowledge that she felt was necessary. The fact that this person woke up feeling fearful and upset indicates that there was likely a situation going on in her life that was causing her to feel inadequate and fearful about not having enough experience, knowledge, or wisdom. (This individual was looking for a job after she had finished school and was afraid that she didn't have enough experience to find one.)

✝✝✝

Dream: This individual and her husband were driving a car, and their son was in the passenger seat. This individual, the wife, was in the back seat. A truck came out of the side street and drove into a wall just in front of them. Then those in the truck began edging up the wall as another truck pushed from behind to help the first truck get to the next level. At this point, the dreamer yelled out to her husband to stop the car because the first truck was blocking the road. Finally they stopped the car after it was under the belly of the first truck, and they got out of the car.

154

Symbols: The car, the trucks, the wall in front of them, the crash, and getting out of the car and leaving it.

People: The dreamer, her son, and her husband.

Interpretation: The walls that the trucks were trying to break through represent the barriers that this family and their Ministry had to overcome to get the Ministry started or keep it going. They had received a call to Ministry, and the other trucks represented other Ministries that were bigger than theirs. The fact that the other trucks were trying to push them past the wall indicates that the trucks, or other Ministries, would be involved in trying to help their Ministry survive or to get their Ministry to the next level. The fact that the car ended up under the first truck or Ministry indicates that the first truck would begin helping this smaller Ministry and family to overcome the barriers and actually would end up hurting their Ministry more than helping it. In other words, it would somehow end up blocking this smaller Ministry more than assisting it.

The purpose of this dream was to warn the vessels of this smaller Ministry that unless they do something to change things to limit or eliminate their reliance on the larger Ministry, their Ministry could potentially end up shutting down, causing them to get out of the Ministry. This was symbolized by the fact that they got out of the car.

†††

Dream: this person found herself lifted over a very tall wall, looking through a glass window. Through this wall, she observed a male mistreating a female. The male dragged the female to the water and tried to drown her. The dreamer left the scene to call for help and told others to call

911. However, instead of calling 911, the others dialed 211.

This person remembered feeling like time was running out,

so she ran back to the window to observe what was going

on and saw that the male and female that she saw before

had left, but there were two people at the bottom of the

water who had almost drowned. The dreamer wanted to call

for help for those two people but felt paralyzed because she

could not get the quick help that she needed to save them.

She remembered saying to herself, "I am a witness."

Symbols: 911, 211, telling others to help to call, the wall,

walls being removed.

Feelings: Paralyzed, of being a witness, empowered.

Interpretation: The wall is symbolic of a hindrance or

barrier that this person may have been experiencing in her

life, or beliefs that may be preventing this person from

moving ahead. The fact that the walls were removed

indicates that the barriers or hindrances that have been operating in this person's life will be removed, and once the wall is removed, this person will have a revelation, which was represented by the window.

This dream was communicating that this person has been hindered from taking action due to her belief systems and has been relying on others to take action instead, which has led to disappointment. This person was obviously not comfortable taking action on her own and was more comfortable having other people do for them what they were being called to do. This person was likely prophetic and would receive a revelation.

†††

Again, this is just a small sample of some dreams

and examples of how to break down a dream, and then how to pull it all together and interpret the dream. Though I wasn't able to demonstrate the implementation of the Holy Spirit, in breaking it down, regardless of what you do before interpreting, you must *include* the Holy Spirit by asking the Holy Spirit for wisdom and faith in going forth and interpreting the dream.

The last important thing to remember is to never take the dreams out of context; the Holy Spirit helps with the dreams and context, so if you don't know the full context, you may always rely on the wisdom of the Holy Spirit.

Chapter Sixteen: Bonus Chapter

Lucid Dreaming, Dream Work, and Reentering your

Dreams

Changing The Course of Your Life While You're Asleep

Have you ever had a dream in which you realized that you were dreaming during your dream? Have you ever taken authority of your response to an event, person, or circumstance in your dream and changed the outcome of the dream? If you answered yes to any of the above questions, you have had what is called a lucid dream. Lucid dreaming is defined as the experience of being conscious or aware that you are dreaming, while you are dreaming. When we're asleep, our bodies are inactive, our physical senses are shut down, and we are closed to the physical realm as we know it; however, our soul and spirit continue to communicate with us to enlighten us regarding things that may be adversely affecting our soul or things that God wants to communicate to us about our decisions, purpose, future, relationships, communion with Him, etc.

Although it appears that our dreams and sleep life are not as powerful, significant, or meaningful as our waking hours, this is an issue that is definitely debatable. In our waking life, we have the opportunity to evaluate life situations and decide on our response. Our response is often determined by our thoughts and beliefs; as Proverbs 23:7 states, *"For as a man thinks in his heart, so is he."* In other words, the thoughts and beliefs that are on our subconscious, that we truly believe, will determine who we are and the outcome of our lives. I believe that God gives us opportunities to change the course of our lives or our thinking while we're awake or while we're sleeping. One

161

example of this is the aforementioned lucid dreaming. Dreams include symbolic content *and* our response to them. If God is communicating a problematic issue in our lives, the dream may convey our previous response, or the outcome if we continue to respond in a particular way.

Nevertheless, in a dream, since our conscious self or ego is asleep and we are operating in the spirit realm, we have the opportunity to respond to a situation or experience that mimics situations or experiences that we may be encountering in our physical or waking life. In other words, we have the opportunity to activate faith and confidence in overcoming obstacles in our dreams, and consequently gain this same sense of confidence and faith as we approach our real life situations. The goal is to generalize the action of overcoming the obstacles of fears, doubts, circumstances, etc. and take this experience from the Spiritual realm while we're asleep, to the physical realm while we're awake. God wants us to be empowered and full of faith so that we will be able to overcome any situation or circumstance that we encounter, and He does not limit Himself to communicating with us while we're awake.

The book of Daniel 7 demonstrates this concept, which Pastor Pugh from Livingstone Church in Aurora calls "Reentry." In Daniel 7:1, Daniel had a dream, wrote the main facts of the dream down, and then had visions about the same dream. The visions elaborated on the dream and even clarified some parts of it.

In Daniel 7:2, Daniel states, *"I was looking into my vision by night (dream) and behold the four winds of heaven were stirring up the great sea."* Daniel had a dream, woke up from the dream, and searched for meaning about the dream. He re-entered (or re-experienced) the same dream and was lucid, because he knew he was dreaming. According to Pastor Pugh of Livingstone Christian Ministries, Daniel was able to interpret his dream by taking four specific steps.

1. Dream Reentry, which entailed Daniel intentionally and consciously going back into the dream to examine the content and meaning of the dream.

2. Re-animation, which entailed the dream coming to life and allowing the imagination to re-experience the dream, its content and meaning.

3. Contemplation, which included meditating on the dream to increase revelation.

4. Interviewing Dream Characters to help to gain understanding and interpretation of the dream. In Daniel 7:16, Daniel asked a character in his dream

for interpretation and the character gave him the interpretation.

Daniel's dream reentry begins with him remembering or looking back into his dream images. Daniel looks at his journal to remember the details, or, if it's still fresh in his mind, he simply brings the dream images back to his remembrance until the dream is reanimated or comes to life again, and then he permits his imagination to revisit and re-experience the content of the dream. As he revisits the dream, he begins to deeply meditate on the dream to expand revelation. Once he reenters the dream, he approaches some of the individuals or bystanders in his dream and begins asking them questions about the interpretation of his dream. One of them provides him with the requested interpretation.

Daniel started with his dream journal, the main facts of his dream, the Holy Spirit, and his imagination, and he concluded with a very detailed, revealing, and life-changing explanation of his dream. This powerful concept and revelation expands our understanding of dreams and reveals extraordinary possibilities. If we are willing to diligently record and press in to our dreams, we may be able to continue to gather understanding and revelation from our dreams even after waking up. We may be able to re-experience dreams that have had a significant impact on our night life and could potentially impact our day life.

This book is to inform you and empower you to take authority of your life while you're awake *and* while you're sleeping. The Bible says in Hosea 4: 6, *"My people are destroyed for lack of knowledge."* Apply the knowledge that you have learned in the past chapters to overcome unnecessary challenges and obstacles in your life.

Conclusion

There are thousands of scientific explanations for the phenomenon that is dreaming, and none of them are concrete. Consciousness and the subconscious are still, and probably always will be, the greatest mystery of science itself. For this reason, we're all fallible in our dream interpretation efforts; however, I believe that using the Holy Spirit as our guide, teacher, and counselor significantly decreases room for human error. The truth is, the study of dreams reaches many solid conclusions about the science of sleeping, but not as many solid conclusions for dreaming or interpreting dreams.

Our Christian beliefs and what we know to be scientific law are often at odds, but dreaming is one of the many aspects of life that science cannot factually explain.

169

On the subject of dreaming, it might be best if we think with our faith first, and science second.

Taking our faith into account first as it pertains to dreaming is important when observing all of the biblical occurrences that were either a direct or indirect result of dreams, and the interpretation of these dreams. The most notable example, of course, is Israel's son Joseph, who became one of the most powerful men in the ancient world because of his uncanny ability to not only correctly interpret his own dreams, but interpret those of others in ways that could predict the future. The second most notable example is the Book of Revelation itself; its title alone signifies that everything we learn during the Book of Revelation is a vision. However, the Book of Revelation is remarkable in that it isn't our dream or vision; rather, we are to learn from this vision, and experience it and understand it as St. John has. The Book of Revelation is a dream, a cautionary tale, a nightmare, a night terror, a prophecy, a condemnation, an apocalyptic vision, and a beacon of hope that is an experience all Christians who read the book must share. The New Testament, and maybe even the Bible itself, would be incomplete without the Book of Revelation, especially for those of us who consider the Bible to be the Old Testament as the past of mankind, the majority of the New Testament to be the Biblical present of mankind, and The Book of Revelation to be the future of mankind.

As we've seen in previous chapters, the Bible is filled with instances where dreams made a difference, and there are even a few situations that seemed real but might have occurred in the form of dreams to those whom experienced them.

The nature of dreams makes anything possible. What is certain is that God speaks to us all if we're willing to listen. The old adage "The Lord works in mysterious ways" is a fact, as God speaks to us through pleasing and unpleasing events in our lives, through people, through places, and yes, through our dreams. While we may sometimes realize when God is trying to tell us something in our waking state, how God speaks to us in our sleeping state can be a lot harder. It's believed by some that things which take place in our dreams are useless, but I assure you that just as everything in waking life has purpose no matter how minor it is, everything in dreams has meaning. Everything.

I pray that this book has answered many of your questions related to dreams and dream interpretation, as many of the questions that I've answered are the same questions I've asked myself concerning dreams, my life as a Christian, and both combined. I've found answers to so many of life's questions within the Gospels, but still many more questions remain. More than I'll ever have answered in a lifetime, some may not be answered until I go to be with God. But if I can answer a few questions, or at least offer a few explanations concerning why God has given us the joy of dreams and what they mean, I'd be able go to God just a little more content in knowing that I passed some of that information on.

Dream Consultation or Presentation

Lisa Kohut does personal dream consultations by phone and provides dream interpretation presentations at different sites.

➤ If you would like to request a dream consultation please go to www.godlydreams.com or call 847-845-2092.

➤ If you would like to request a dream interpretation presentation at your site please contact Lisa Kohut at 847-845-2092.

Eternal Life Prayer

If you read this book and you have decided that you would like the certainty of eternal life by accepting Jesus Christ into your heart, read the following prayer out loud:

"Lord Jesus Christ, I know I am a sinner and do not deserve eternal life. But I believe that you died and rose from the grave to purchase a place in Heaven for me. Lord Jesus, come into my life; take control of my life; forgive my sins and save me. I repent of my sins and now place my trust in You for my salvation. I accept the free gift of eternal life."

Prayer for the Power of the Holy Spirit

If you have already prayed the eternal life prayer and you have decided that you would like to activate the power of the Holy Spirit in your life, then pray the following prayer:

"Lord Jesus, I thank You for the most exciting gift on earth, the gift of salvation and eternal life. Jesus, You promised another gift; the gift of the Holy Spirit. So I ask You, Lord Jesus, to baptize me with the Holy Spirit right now, exactly like on the Day of Pentecost. Thank you, Jesus. Lift your hands up to God and in Faith, begin to make sounds out loud."

References for *Dreams Mysteries: Secrets to Interpreting Your Dreams to Know God's Purpose for Your Life*

1. Hamon, Jane. (2000). *Dreams and Visions*. Regal Books, Ventura, CA. *Dreams and Visions* was originally published by Christian Int'l Ministries in 1997.

2. Hayford, Jack W., Chappel, Paul, & Ulmer, Kenneth, C. *The Holy Bible, New King James Version*. (2002). Thomas Nelson Bibles, Nashville, TN.

3. Goll, James W. and Michal Ann. (2006). *Dream Language: The Prophetic Power of Dreams, Revelations, and the Spirit of Wisdom*. Destiny Image Publishers, Inc., Shippensburg, PA.

4. Ibojie, Dr. Joe (2005) The Illustrated Bible-Based Dictionary of Dream Symbols. Destiny Image Publishers, Inc., Europe.

5. Pugh, R. (1990). *Dreams &Visions Student's Manual*. Capstone Christian Ministries, Int'l. Aurora, IL.

6. Pugh, R. (2006). *Understanding Your Dreams & Visions*. Capstone Christian Ministries, Int'l., Aurora, IL.

7. Virkler, Mark & Patti. (2005). *How to Hear God's Voice*. Destiny Image Publishers, Inc., Shippensburg, PA.

8000296R0

Made in the USA
Charleston, SC
29 April 2011